5|24|18
$29.99

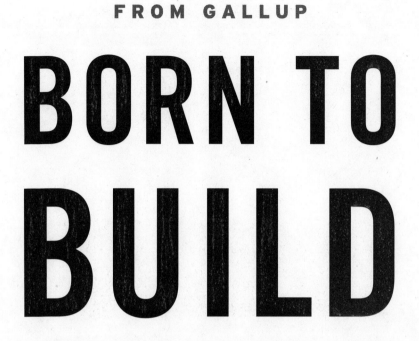

FROM GALLUP

BORN TO BUILD

HOW TO BUILD A THRIVING STARTUP, A
WINNING TEAM, NEW CUSTOMERS AND
YOUR BEST LIFE IMAGINABLE

JIM CLIFTON
Chairman of Gallup

SANGEETA BADAL, Ph.D.

GALLUP PRESS
1330 Avenue of the Americas
17th Floor
New York, NY 10019

Library of Congress Control Number: 2017963448
ISBN: 978-1-59562-127-6

First Printing: 2018
10 9 8 7 6 5 4 3 2 1

Printed in Canada

♻ This book was printed on chlorine-free paper made with 100% post-consumer waste.

TO THOSE WHO BUILD THE WORLD

– JIM

TO MY PARENTS AND
TO MY TEACHER, DR. STODDARD

– SANGEETA

Table of Contents

Part One:

WHAT ARE YOU BUILDING?

People will ask you throughout your life, "Where do you work?" and "What do you do?" They never ask you, "What are you building?"

When conversations change to "What are you building?" you will change, and so will the world.

Well-meaning and important global institutions, scientists, academics and politicians have never fully understood the rare gift to build something — a God-given natural talent that many are born with — that to some degree, you yourself possess.

Some refer to this gift as "entrepreneurship," which it is, in part. But this human phenomenon is better characterized as "building." Entrepreneurship has taken on many definitions, and it's often confused with innovation. We need a lot of innovation, but building is a very distinct, separate phenomenon.

An innovation has no value until an ambitious builder creates a business model around it and turns it into a product or service that customers will buy.

An innovator is first and foremost a creator, an inventor — a problem solver with a deep passion for improving something. Innovators are thinkers.

A builder is different from an innovator. A builder creates economic energy where none previously existed.

Builders can start very young. When an 8-year-old puts a lemonade stand on a corner, they create new economic energy on that corner — goods and services are exchanged for the first time at that place. Years ago, a 14-year-old could take on an existing newspaper delivery route with 25 papers and boom it to 100 papers. This young builder created economic energy that wasn't on that route before. Believe it or not, U.S. GDP actually ticked up a little when that paper route quadrupled.

Builders also create goods and services that customers didn't even know they wanted or had ever imagined. Builders create demand. When Google or Apple was launched or the first commercial airplane took off in 1914, there was no inherent demand for any of their products or services. Nobody said, "Gee, I wish I had a device in my pocket on which I could search everything humans have recorded since the beginning of time instead of going to a library."

Or, "It would be so cool to fly through the air in a metal tube at 400 mph rather than ride to my destination on my horse."

Or, "I wish someone would invent plumbing and electricity rather than using candles and kerosene — and going to the toilet outside."

Economists and well-meaning thinkers often look at a weak or declining economy and conclude, "We have a declining economy because demand is weak or because there is no demand at all." A more insightful observation is, "There is no demand because there aren't enough builders who *create demand*." Without builders, there is no demand, no growing economy and hence, no good jobs.

There was never an inherent demand for cars, flight, TV, video, indoor plumbing, electricity or the internet, or Starbucks or Amazon — somebody had to take a good idea and build it into something big. And when people do that, they create economic energy that wasn't there before — as well as new good jobs and all the things that build a growing economy.

Is it time for you to think about building something? Maybe you could build a small or medium-sized business. Or build a huge business — one with $10 million or $10 billion in sales. They all count and add up to the sum total of the world economy. We need hundreds of thousands of small and medium-sized businesses. All societies need organizations of all kinds continuously starting up and booming — or they can't develop.

You can do this.

You could also build a small, medium or jumbo nonprofit. Nonprofits create economic energy too. They boost GDP and create real jobs and real growth in cities and states. So do megachurches, a new children's museum, a chain of daycare centers, home-health nonprofits or charities to assist disadvantaged citizens. Every one of these organizations or institutions requires a business model and a gifted builder or they will never take off — they will never create new economic energy in the absence of a born builder.

You could become an "intrapreneur" too.

Intrapreneurs are people who build startups inside established organizations — people who are given hard assignments to start new ventures inside an institution. Established organizations like Gallup will assign someone to "go start a new division that will sell millions of books" or "start a new analytics division" or "start a new center that specifically serves colleges and universities" or "go open a new office in Dubai or Seoul." These jobs require builders.

Building is a high-degree-of-difficulty task, but natural builders want the impossible assignment. They actually prefer the messiness, the problems, the barriers, the absence of supervision, the improvisation and the rush of a new customer breakthrough.

Builders are made differently than the rest of us. They are born and put on earth to build.

Are you a builder?

Builders from Andrew Carnegie to J.P. Morgan to John D. Rockefeller to Henry Ford famously created historic economic energy through steel, electricity, trains and cars. They transformed America and the world because they created *customers* that didn't previously exist. They had a gift to envision, create masses of customers and change how we live. They also made very big bets — they would sometimes bet everything they were worth. Extreme builders will, a few times in their life, bet it all.

Every institution in the world — even nonprofits, schools and churches — has customers. Builders are born with a gift to know how to create demand for those customers — market disruptions that offer a better way to live.

Jack Dorsey and his Twitter co-founders didn't respond to a market demand. They disrupted the media market and created a different way to communicate and socialize.

John built a large nonprofit organization to help low-income people improve their credit scores so they could immediately improve their lives. He created a quick education course on money and credit available at a special desk in bank branches throughout the country. Millions of low-income Americans needed this service. John's paying customers are the financial institutions because they primarily fund his nonprofit. It is extremely valuable for banks to have citizens who have good credit versus bad or mistakenly low credit scores.

Banks weren't clamoring for this, and many low-income people hadn't even imagined this type of service. John built a huge nationwide nonprofit through envisioning two customers — the low-income citizens who use the service (for free) and the secondary customers, the banks, who fund it. John created customers and economic energy where it hadn't previously existed. He improved lives and changed the world.

Roy and some of his college friends co-founded an ad agency after attending the University of Texas at Austin in 1971. His agency was going to be different from others because rather than simply focusing on traditional branding and marketing, Roy's agency would help customers identify their values and purpose — and communicate to the world *why* they were in business. Values and purpose, not just positioning and brand differentiation, would drive all of his firm's creative work for clients. And the approach proved to be a huge success. Roy became famous for his "purpose-inspired branding," and the firm he and his partners built boasted big clients such as Walmart, Southwest Airlines and the U.S. Air Force.

Roy has since passed the torch with his firm, but he can't stop building. He has built the Purpose Institute and has started selling his own brand of Royito's Hot Sauce from an Airstream breakfast food truck where he himself works.

Roy's purpose in life is to help others fulfill their purpose. He always says to young people, "You can make a living and a life becoming great at what you are already good at — and spending your life doing what you love to do." Doing just that is in Roy's DNA.

Emily was a student at George Washington University in Washington, D.C. She joined a national nonprofit, Lemonade Day, and took on the challenge of founding a Lemonade Day chapter on the GWU campus.

Lemonade Day teaches fifth- through eighth-graders how to run a business — in this case, their own lemonade stand — and they get to keep the profits. Emily is a born builder, and, with funding, she quickly built a nonprofit that recruits, trains and transports approximately 500 college students a year to mentor 8,000 elementary and middle school students.

She built a nonprofit colossus as a full-time student. New energy exploded from the fifth- through eighth-graders, the college students who received college credit and the local businesses who funded it.

Lemonade Day also created a large-scale mentorship model for universities for its national program. This has inspired universities to adopt this model and bring Lemonade Day to their city through university students.

Emily is a born builder. When she rises in the morning, she sees her world through the lens of "What can I build today?"

John and Jim borrowed $5,000 40 years ago to start a small Midwest market research company. They built it because they wanted to do something on their own. They didn't want entry-level sales jobs at IBM or Xerox, which were the hottest jobs on earth back then.

Like most builders, John and Jim got up every morning to build something because they were primarily driven by a need — not so much for money but a need for independence and extreme individualism. They found a highly inspiring job by building their own enterprise, which, with their colleagues, they are still building and growing today.

But creating a big booming enterprise or nonprofit organization won't happen with just one gifted builder. There is a fragile ecosystem around effective builders.

Gallup has found that there are three key players in the development of any organization, whether it's a new enterprise, a new division within a company or a nonprofit. We call them the "three alphas": the alpha Rainmaker, the alpha Conductor and the alpha Expert. When this combination exists in an organization or on a team, the likelihood of it breaking out and booming grows exponentially.

An alpha *Rainmaker* has unusual drive and persistence — rare grit. Obstacles and failure actually increase a Rainmaker's determination. An enterprise virtually never works without this player.

An alpha *Conductor* has management ability. This is the operations person or manager who knows how to get all players on the team — or in the "orchestra"— to work together seamlessly. This person holds the whole organization together.

An alpha *Expert* provides differentiating expertise to the core product or service. Whether it is an analytic services startup's brilliant statistician, a new restaurant's star chef or a software firm's best programmer, virtually every successful startup has an alpha expert who highly distinguishes it from the crowd.

Born to Build and the assessment included with it were created to help you decide how building plays into your life and career. They will help you answer the question "Am I an alpha builder?"

The trick is knowing how you fit in. This book will help you determine which alpha role is best for you. It will tell you from which role your God-given strengths will develop most.

There is nothing wrong with wanting to build something big and important that makes you rich and famous — or building something that changes the world a little to a lot. There is nothing wrong with wanting to be a significant person in this world who leaves a lasting legacy. It often comes with being a successful builder.

You were born to do this. Whether you are an alpha Rainmaker, an alpha Conductor or an alpha Expert, there are no limits to what you can build.

Part Two:

THE FOUR KEYS
TO BUILDING

THE BUILDER'S MINDSET

"Where do I begin?" you ask.

Sara asked the same thing. She had tinkered with hardware in her father's garage since she was in high school. She watched him design motors, robotic arms and all sorts of gadgets in his small workshop.

Engineering was her calling. She graduated from college with an electrical engineering degree. Now, Sara has a compelling idea to build solar inverters that convert the electricity generated by solar panels into a form that homeowners can use to run their appliances, lighting and other electronics.

But she has no idea where to begin.

Since graduating eight months ago, Sara has applied to more than 50 engineering firms looking for an entry-level position, but she has not received a single positive response. She is working at the local coffee shop while waiting to land a job. She has also applied to a master's degree program in electrical engineering, just in case she cannot find a job.

Sara is not alone. A 2017 study of recent graduates (aged 22 to 27 with a bachelor's degree or higher) by the Federal Reserve Bank of New York found that 4% are unemployed, and 44% are underemployed. College graduates like Sara are considered underemployed when they settle for jobs that are not full time, do not pay well and, in many cases, do not even require a college degree.

Jobs with benefits and professional and financial security are becoming less common as the labor market moves more toward a "gig" economy — a gradual shift away from conventional 9-to-5 jobs toward alternative work that is flexible and temporary. This change may mark a decline in the kind of steady and stable full-time jobs people have grown accustomed to and the beginning of a new work era in the U.S. and around the world.

Those who want to survive and succeed in the shifting employment landscape must bring resourcefulness, optimism, pragmatism and resilience to the table. Enterprising qualities such as initiative, innovation, creativity, risk-taking, and the ability to sell ideas or products are highly desirable in this fluid work environment.

Gallup's advice to young people looking for jobs, employees looking to advance their careers or retirees beginning an encore career is: Embrace the shift! Cultivate the mindset of a builder — it is key to your success.

Successful builders proactively develop behaviors that empower them to anticipate problems, overcome adversity, recognize opportunities, organize resources and take action to build something. Understanding and developing such behaviors is invaluable, regardless of the career or personal path you pursue.

A recent study conducted by Francisco Campos from the World Bank and a team of researchers found that a psychology-based training program that develops entrepreneurial behaviors among small-business owners increased firm profits by 30%, compared with just 11% for a group that had traditional business training. In the pages ahead, we discuss a psychologically driven approach to cultivating the mindset of a builder.

Whether you are a dentist building a practice, a pastor building a congregation, a chef building a restaurant, a student building a startup, a coder building a mobile app or a corporate executive building a new line of business, the process of building something for a customer creates value and spurs economic growth. But more importantly, it makes life deeply satisfying and gives it meaning and purpose.

14

Humans are born to build. People seek fulfillment, engagement and meaning in life. Everyone has the seed of a builder inside them, expressed through the hobbies and passions they pursue throughout their lives.

Building something that is meaningful and fulfilling for you starts a process of learning and building skills, increases your self-efficacy, helps you achieve mastery in a particular area, and increases your motivation and engagement. You become an engine of entrepreneurial innovation that powers your economy.

And there are plenty of sources of inspiration: rags-to-riches stories of highly successful builders; pioneers who create something from scratch, with barely any resources, and build multimillion-dollar ventures in just a few years; lone inventors in garages who hustle their way to success; and individuals who faced repeated rejections and obstacles before reaching the heights of achievement.

There are many stories of highly successful builders who not only were the first to recognize opportunities in their environment, but in many cases, they outright created new opportunities for themselves. They were not passive bystanders waiting for opportunities to emerge. Rather, their behaviors, actions and thought processes shaped an environment from which new opportunities emerged. They created new customers where none existed and opened up new markets that no one anticipated.

For instance, when John Leguizamo, the theater and film actor, tried to find work in films and TV in the 1980s, his options were limited. There was very little work available to Latino artists. After multiple rejections and some forgettable roles, Leguizamo decided to build a theater for himself — a stage where he could show his craft and be taken seriously as an artist. He wrote and staged his first play, *Mambo Mouth*, in 1990, which opened to an audience of 70 people.

Twenty-five years later, he is still writing and building his own roles. Even as opportunities in film and TV have expanded, he continues to write and perform on stage about issues that are deeply important to him.

Leguizamo didn't wait for roles to fall into his lap. He built roles for himself. He is a builder who used his personal history and his desire to bring to life something close to his heart. He closed the gap between his actual reality (*what is*) and his desired situation (*what should be*).

Dave Myers was another builder who opened up a new market for his employer. Myers was an engineer at W.L. Gore & Associates, a global material science company. His full-time work was developing plastic heart implants at the medical product plant in Flagstaff, Arizona, but he tinkered with his mountain bike gears in his spare time. He used a polymer (a Teflon-like material) developed by his company to coat the gears of his bike with the hope that it would improve the bike's movement.

Myers' tinkering resulted in a new line of business for Gore: Ride On cable systems for bicycles. Though Gore discontinued the product, Myers continued developing his idea of coating cables and strings with the stretched polymer to make them stronger and improve their performance.

During one of his experiments, it struck him that coating guitar strings with this polymer might improve their durability and performance. He sought the help of a colleague who was an avid guitarist. His colleague confirmed that guitar strings lose their tonal quality due to accumulation of dirt and oils from regular use.

Myers persuaded others in the company to join him in his efforts. After three years of development, the team got approval from senior management, and they launched Elixir strings. Elixir strings have superior tonal quality and last three times longer than regular strings. Today, Elixir is the leading brand of acoustic guitar strings, with a 35% market share in the U.S.

Myers did not passively wait for opportunities to further his career at Gore. He created a new product for his company from a side project — fixing his mountain bike. In the process, he opened up a new market for Gore that no one had anticipated.

When Charles Schwab launched one of the first discount brokerage firms in the U.S., which today oversees $2.5 trillion in net assets, the financial industry was in turmoil due to a major regulatory change by the Securities and Exchange Commission (SEC). In 1975, the SEC eliminated the practice of fixed brokerage commissions, which required investors to pay a fixed fee for a typical trade.

As the financial industry vigorously opposed the regulatory change — making dire predictions of the downfall of the free enterprise system — Schwab saw a unique opportunity to make the world of investing more accessible to the individual investor. There was a market waiting to be tapped that none of the major brokerage firms had anticipated at the time.

Schwab's entrepreneurial actions in the face of regulatory changes in his environment revolutionized and disrupted the brokerage industry. His actions led to the emergence of a new market — unleashing innovation in technology and spawning new services and pricing in the financial world.

As inspiring as Leguizamo's, Myers' and Schwab's stories can be, they are a bit overwhelming for the individual who knows nothing about building a venture. You are not alone if you're asking yourself:

- **Do I have what it takes to build?**
  "I don't have a degree from Oxford or Yale."

- **What should I build?**
  "I don't have a multimillion-dollar or world-changing idea."

- **Where do I begin?**
  "I don't have a clue!"

- **Whom do I ask for help?**
  "I don't know anyone who has built something from scratch."

Each question and concern becomes a potential minefield — a hurdle in the path of building.

To help you navigate the process of building, this book outlines a method you can learn and use to build your future — a proven set of techniques that can help you see or even create opportunities for yourself. Using these techniques, you will learn how to take logical steps toward building something.

Instead of looking for that elusive job, following the traditional career path or waiting endlessly for the next promotion, you can learn to proactively build your own future. You can cultivate the mindset of a successful builder.

The Four Keys to Building

It is essential to study the actions and decision-making processes of successful builders to decode the builder's method. So Gallup studied over 4,000 entrepreneurs and more than 30,000 non-entrepreneurs. We conducted focus groups, asked questions and listened intently as highly successful builders explained what they do and how they do it.

We asked stakeholders, policymakers and support providers what it takes to build something that is sustainable and creates economic value. We collected and analyzed data on some exceptional builders of the U.S. economy — such as the Inc. 500, with an average three-year growth rate of over 3,300% — as well as others that started small and had every intention of staying small.

Borrowing ideas from recent developments in the fields of economics, psychology, biology, anthropology, sociology and management, we put together a toolkit that makes the process of building accessible to everyone — not only the select few who decide to start a venture. This toolkit is a way of thinking, assessing problems and finding solutions — a mindset that you can apply to all spheres of your life.

You may decide to build a small, medium or large business; a thriving division within a big company; a nonprofit; a church; a camp; or a school.

We are going to help you think like a builder so you can build your future, regardless of what that future is, with the four keys to building:

- **Creating Self-Awareness:** The first step is "know thyself." Being aware of your capabilities, motivations and feelings will lead to psychological clarity and better outcomes. Gallup research indicates that as individuals attain psychological clarity, they gain confidence in their ability to build new ventures. In this section of the book, you will read about gaining that clarity and answer the question "Do I have what it takes to build?" You will also learn what type of alpha builder you are — Rainmaker, Conductor or Expert — based on your talents.

- **Recognizing Opportunities:** This section of the book outlines the path to opportunity recognition and helps you answer the question "What should I build?" Opportunities are all around you. Some are visible — such as a process that needs to be improved or a gap in *what is* versus *what should be* that triggers an idea. Others are waiting for you to discover them — for example, new developments in technology or industry, changes in regulations or institutions (like the ones Charles Schwab encountered), unexpected events, or demographic shifts that bring up new opportunities that no one anticipates. Digging deep within yourself and into your immediate environment, you will learn how to discover and identify opportunities.

- **Activating on Ideas:** Ideas mean nothing without action. In this section of the book, we outline the process of building your idea into a product, service or solution. You will answer the question "Where do I begin?" and break the process into small steps. By learning how to create *minimally viable solutions* to the problem you want to solve, how to find your first strategic partner (i.e., your first customer) and how to test-drive your ideas, you can take your first steps with confidence.

- **Building a Team:** In this section of the book, we discuss the importance of talent distribution on teams rather than having one "ideal" builder. Research indicates that successful builders rely on their social networks. They co-create with their customers. They build alliances with their suppliers and investors to reduce uncertainty and bring their ideas to market. You will explore how to use a talent-based perspective to create a well-rounded team that includes a Rainmaker, Conductor and Expert. You will also learn how to build an extended team that includes various stakeholders and partners who are invested in your success.

Use this book as a manual. Ask your co-founders, employers and others who are helping you build to read it too so you can discuss your progress and challenges with them. Each section has hands-on exercises to guide you through the process of building something from scratch. Make sure to do all the exercises in each section. They will help you navigate the unknowns of starting something new by helping you become self-aware, discover opportunities, build and test your hypotheses, find your customers, and build your team.

We hope that the techniques in this book clarify who you are, what you can build and how — and that by following them, you will be empowered to build a sustainable, profitable and scalable venture.

Every builder will carve their own journey. But regardless of where you are in the process of building a venture, we strongly recommend that you start with the first key, **Creating Self-Awareness**. This is the primary building block of being a successful builder. If you already have an idea that is keeping you up at night, then skip the second key, **Recognizing Opportunities**, and move to the next key, **Activating on Ideas**, to test your hypotheses with your very first customers. If your venture is well under way, you might want to jump to the fourth key, **Building a Team**.

Remember, no book can give you all the answers and solve all your problems. The path we have sketched out shows you the way, but the journey is yours.

If you are an investor, coach, mentor, city leader or company leader who has a stake in a builder's success, you can identify, develop and support the budding talent of those who want to build something. Educators who want to teach others how to start a venture can find additional resources and links to digital content on our website. You can organize each chapter into a lecture with hands-on exercises for your students.

The builder way of thinking is an essential life skill. You can become a builder if you choose to by developing your natural talents such as determination, personal initiative or creative thinking and learning and applying the strategies in this book.

Whether you're a new employee looking for career growth and engagement, a manager who wants to create jobs or build your own future, an inventor who wants to improve the lives of others, or an individual with a mission to save the world or the local economy — we encourage you to develop your ideas, build something, create a business model and find a customer.

This book gives you the tools you need to build a future that is financially secure, emotionally rewarding and purpose-filled.

There is a lot to do. Let's get started.

THE FIRST KEY:
CREATING SELF-AWARENESS

Building a small business, a social enterprise, a high-growth technology venture or a new division in an established organization takes vision and action. You gather and organize resources, produce and market products or services in untested markets, find and retain customers, and figure out how to scale and grow — often with scarce resources and a low probability of success. As a builder, you will face immense challenges and confront uncertain situations.

Facing these challenges successfully requires a high level of awareness of your innate talents. How do you think, reason and make decisions? What is your failure-tolerance level? How determined are you in the face of obstacles? The answers lie in understanding yourself.

Just like John Leguizamo's path to building his theater roles was deeply rooted in his Latino identity, being aware of who you are and what your beliefs, innate capabilities and values are will lead to psychological clarity and enable you to take action. Who you are will permeate the decisions you make, the routines you establish, the teams you create and the ventures you build. So ask yourself, "Given who I am, what kind of builder can I be? What kind of opportunities can I explore that best suit me? What can I build that resonates deeply with who I am?"

What Evidence Do We Have?

As far back as the 1930s, economists like Irving Fisher and John Maynard Keynes have studied the link between individual characteristics and economic behavior. Since then, research has clearly established positive significant relationships between certain psychological traits (talents) — e.g., risk propensity, creativity, determination and self-efficacy — and several life outcomes such as personal well-being and engagement at work as well as hard-core business outcomes like sales growth, number of employees hired, number of new products introduced or growth in profit.

Gallup defines talent as the natural capacity for excellence in a role. Talents are recurring patterns of thought, feeling and behavior that are enduring and stable over time and across situations. Talent is a broader concept than personality traits. It is a composite of basic personality traits and cognitive abilities. Personality traits can be talents, but not all talents are personality traits. The talents we measure include personality traits but also thinking styles, for example, which overlap with general mental ability/intelligence.

Through our assessment of individual potential, we can determine if an individual possesses a critical mass of talent relative to the typical characteristics of the most successful builders, then predict if that individual is more likely to naturally and consistently behave in ways that lead to excellence in the role. For example, some people are naturally more creative, some are adept at managing risk and some have very high levels of self-confidence. These talents affect their behaviors, which in turn, affect outcomes such as business survival or growth.

Note that though talents show a high degree of stability over time, they can evolve or change in certain situations. Some parts of personality are more malleable. That is, they can change easier than others. For the most part though, talents are stable over time and can be used to predict behaviors in a wide variety of situations.

Here are a few examples of the *talent-behavior-outcome* link that have been scientifically studied and proven to influence business building and success:

- Creativity *talent* is the natural ability to think of novel ways to do things. Cumulative evidence indicates that *behaviors* associated with creativity include the ability to generate many different ideas, quickly switch from one perspective to another and make unusual associations between ideas. *Outcomes*: People with creativity talent bring new solutions, new products, new services or new processes to existing markets. **Gallup research finds that builders with dominant creativity (Disruptor) talent are three times more likely to hold patents.**

- Risk-taking *talent* is the propensity to pursue an idea when the probability of success is low. Risk-takers exhibit *behaviors* such as a high tolerance for failure, the ability to make decisions in the midst of uncertainty and an analytical approach to risk mitigation (they weigh all the options, create what-if scenarios and calculate the odds of success before taking action). *Outcomes:* Those with risk-taking talent are likely to invest in new projects and explore new markets, which can lead to higher profitability. **Gallup research finds that builders with dominant Risk talent are five times more likely to have businesses with over $1 million in revenue and four times more likely to have a strong intent to grow their business significantly.**

- Self-efficacy *talent* is a belief in one's ability to do a task well. Researchers at the department of psychology at the University of Giessen, Germany, studied *behaviors* associated with high levels of self-efficacy — strong propensity to take initiative, perseverance in the face of resistance, high hopes for success and experimentation with new things. They found that these behaviors lead to *outcomes* such as starting a venture, increased innovation, and successful navigation through the ups and downs of the business cycle. **Gallup research finds that those high in self-efficacy (Confidence) are three times more likely to hire employees, thus creating jobs.**

As you can see, each talent affects specific business outcomes. Some people may be better at noticing new business opportunities; others might be better at risk management. Some may have the natural confidence and swagger of a salesperson, while others may be adept at finding innovative solutions for existing problems.

Like all builders, you are likely to be most successful when you are working within your natural talents. So what kind of builder are *you*? What are *your* builder talents? Creating self-awareness and knowing your unique traits and behaviors will give you the greatest potential for meaningful and sustainable outcomes.

Identifying Your Builder Talents

In our research, Gallup found a variety of behaviors among successful builders. For instance, highly successful builders effortlessly cultivate deep relationships, are laser-focused on results, are creative problem solvers and are the best spokespeople for their venture.

But after analyzing the data from samples across the U.S., Germany and Mexico and listening to hundreds of hours of interviews, we distilled everything to a list of 10 talents that influence behaviors and best explain the success of a builder. Every builder uses some mix of these 10 talents:

- **CONFIDENCE:** You accurately know yourself and understand others.
- **DELEGATOR:** You recognize that you cannot do everything and are willing to contemplate a shift in style and control.
- **DETERMINATION:** You persevere through difficult and seemingly insurmountable obstacles.

- **DISRUPTOR:** You exhibit creativity in taking an existing idea or product and turning it into something better.

- **INDEPENDENCE:** You do whatever needs to be done to build a successful venture.

- **KNOWLEDGE:** You constantly search for information that is relevant to growing your business.

- **PROFITABILITY:** You make decisions based on observed or anticipated effect on profit.

- **RELATIONSHIP:** You possess high social awareness and an ability to build relationships that are beneficial to your organization's survival and growth.

- **RISK:** You instinctively know how to manage high-risk situations.

- **SELLING:** You are the best spokesperson for your business.

To help you find your unique mix of these 10 talents, Gallup created an online assessment called the Builder Profile 10 (BP10), which is included with this book. If you haven't already done so, take the assessment before reading ahead. You will need the unique access code in the packet at the back of the book to take the assessment.

After you complete the assessment, you will receive a report with your unique builder talent profile. Your report lists the 10 builder talents in rank order based on your responses to the assessment. Focus on your top four talents. These are your *dominant talents*, and they will provide your best opportunity for success. Your report also identifies the type of alpha builder you are likely to be: a Rainmaker, a Conductor or an Expert.

Use your customized results as a guide along your journey. The way you are wired will influence not only what you build, but also how you build it. Your talents are the lens you use to look at the world. They guide how you frame problems and the solutions you generate for those problems, what you see as roadblocks and the methods you use to clear them, how you identify your goals and aspirations, and the route you take to fulfilling them.

Remember, each talent is highly relevant to specific business outcomes — but less so to others. For instance, someone with high Disruptor (creative thinking) talent will make sure their venture stays innovative but will be less likely to think about profitability. Independence talent (need for autonomy) is more related to survival of the venture than it is to its growth. And Risk talent (optimistic perception of risk) is positively related to revenue and growth of the venture but is less likely to affect innovation.

The behaviors associated with the 10 talents of successful builders — the 10 talents that are specifically linked to entrepreneurship — enable builders to meet the demands of the role, which ultimately leads to business success. Once you have your builder profile and know your dominant talents, you can start to think about your own *talent-behavior-outcome* pathways to success.

Pathways From Personality to Business Success

Talent →	Behaviors →	Likely business outcomes
Confidence	▪ Know themselves well ▪ Have strong self-belief ▪ Persuade and influence others	▪ Commercialization of new products ▪ Innovation ▪ Early movers in the market
Delegator	▪ Easily delegate authority ▪ Collaborate proactively ▪ Recognize team strengths	▪ Engaged and motivated employees ▪ Higher productivity
Determination	▪ Have a tremendous work ethic ▪ Are tenacious and persistent ▪ Can overcome obstacles	▪ Opportunity recognition ▪ Startup creation ▪ Attainment of business goals
Disruptor	▪ Think outside the box ▪ Imagine possible futures	▪ Business can move in new direction ▪ Market disruption

Pathways From Personality to Business Success

Talent →	Behaviors →	Likely business outcomes
Independence	▪ Can single-handedly manage a startup ▪ Autonomously set goals and take action	▪ Startup survival
Knowledge	▪ Constantly search for new information ▪ Obsess about business activity ▪ Value information as an asset	▪ Competitive advantage in the market ▪ Disruptive innovation ▪ Ability to meet ever-changing customer expectations
Profitability	▪ Have sharp business instincts ▪ Set clear goals ▪ Plan growth strategies	▪ High profitability ▪ Efficient business
Relationship	▪ Have high social awareness ▪ Build diverse networks ▪ Attract and maintain partnerships	▪ Access to financial resources ▪ Emotionally engaged customers and employees ▪ Vital information from networks
Risk	▪ Are comfortable with ambiguity ▪ Take a rational approach to decision-making ▪ Embrace challenges enthusiastically	▪ Opportunity recognition ▪ Benefit from market gaps ▪ New initiatives
Selling	▪ Are ambassadors and evangelists ▪ Persuade others easily ▪ Communicate clearly	▪ Long-term customer commitment ▪ Financial resources for the organization ▪ Distinct identity of business

As part of our research, Gallup asked entrepreneurs the following questions about their revenue; growth goals; how many businesses they have started; plans for growing their employee base; and their copyright, trademark and patent ownership. See the Appendix for response options and more information about this survey.

Q1. What is the current revenue in your most recent business? (in U.S. dollars)

Q2. Thinking ahead to the next five years, which of the following best describes your revenue goals for your business?

Q3. How many businesses have you started, regardless of whether they are still in operation?

Q4. In the next 12 months, by what percentage do you expect to increase or decrease the number of employees?

Q5. Does your current business own one or more of the following (copyright, patent, trademark)?

Based on the entrepreneurs' responses, we found compelling relationships between psychological contexts (dominant builder talents) and business outcomes. For example, those with dominant Profitability talent are five times more likely to have a business with $1 million in revenue and four times more likely to plan to grow their business significantly.

REVENUE

Entrepreneurs with dominant ...

Profitability talent are **5x**

Risk talent are **5x**

Delegator talent are **3x**

Selling talent are **3x**

Independence talent are **2x**

... more likely to have a business with $1 million in revenue

GROWTH

Entrepreneurs with dominant ...

Profitability talent are **4x**

Risk talent are **4x**

Confidence talent are **3x**

Relationship talent are **2x**

... more likely to plan to grow their business significantly

SERIAL ENTREPRENEUR

Entrepreneurs with dominant ...

Risk talent are **3.5x**

Disruptor talent are **2x**

... more likely to plan to start three or more businesses

JOB CREATION

Entrepreneurs with dominant ...

Determination talent are **3.5x**

Confidence talent are **3x**

Independence talent are **3x**

Knowledge talent are **3x**

Delegator talent are **2.5x**

Relationship talent are **2x**

... more likely to plan to increase their employee base by more than 5%

INNOVATION

Entrepreneurs with dominant ...

Disruptor talent are **3x**

... more likely to file for or receive a patent

As you can see, the 10 builder talents influence business outcomes like revenue, growth, job creation and innovation differently. So focus your energy on developing your dominant builder talents — the top four talents on your customized report. Learn how to apply your talents to be the best builder you can be. Use them to your advantage. They are the key to the survival and success of your venture.

Also be aware of your weaknesses or challenges. Manage them by implementing systems, acquiring skills and knowledge, or establishing complementary partnerships. For example, if building relationships is your forte but focusing on business or sales is not, put your energy into forming and cultivating networks that can propel you to the next level — and leave sales and numbers to someone who is better at them.

Rainmakers, Conductors and Experts

Now that you know your top talents, you can figure out what they tell you about the type of builder you are. As we noted earlier, Gallup has identified three types of alpha builders: Rainmakers, Conductors and Experts. Your responses to the BP10 assessment will identify which of these roles you are best suited for.

RAINMAKER: If you are a Rainmaker, you are primarily focused on generating sales and revenue for your venture. You are boldly self-confident in your capacity to be successful, and you rarely miss a moneymaking opportunity. You have a clear and aggressive growth strategy, and you measure success by the profitability of your venture. Incredibly persuasive, you know how to energize customers and employees with your vision of the future. It is easy for you to influence others to accept your point of view.

As a master promoter, you excel at sales and marketing, and you love being the voice and face of your company and pushing your products and services.

While fully self-reliant, you build purposeful connections with others who can help you achieve your goals. Your ability to form authentic relationships with customers and employees helps you further your business objectives.

You display a singular commitment to take on challenges and the risks that come with initiative. You have an optimistic perception of risk. In other words, you perceive potential threats positively, and you take an analytical approach to manage risks.

Your intense drive and ability to take decisive action and manage risks combine to shape your success. Day-to-day management of the business, however, is not something you enjoy — so let others handle the details.

CONDUCTOR: You possess great management talent and mainly focus on the operations of your venture. Like a conductor who unifies an orchestra to produce beautiful music, you bring order and harmony to the chaos of a young venture. You build an organization by building its people. You rarely act alone, and you take pride in finding the right people for key positions. Trusting others to take responsibility, you look for ways to delegate work and authority. You are quick to recognize when someone else can do a job better, and you give them freedom to make decisions and accomplish tasks. You use delegation and relationships as your tools to build capacity in the organization.

You are demanding and have a tendency to challenge the status quo. With little self-doubt, you do not hesitate to decide and act on your own, regardless of what others think.

Your persistence generates trust among your peers, employees and customers. You make a plan, stick with it and don't give up. You feel strongly about keeping promises. When something needs to be done, you make sure it happens, even if something gets in the way.

But your determination and energetic drive are not thoughtless or stubborn. You have the capacity to re-evaluate what you need to achieve your goals. You know when to stay the course and when to reconsider your options.

Hard work energizes you. You believe in high-growth businesses. You are fixated on growth metrics and hold yourself and your team accountable for the goals you set for the venture.

EXPERT: As an Expert, you primarily focus on product development and research for your venture. Being the best in your field in crucial for you. You set the bar high for yourself and focus on breakthrough discoveries. Whether you invent something new or improve a product or service through several iterations, you focus on finding solutions to the issues your customers face. You keep them feeling positive about your organization. In fact, your work helps the organization find new customers.

Highly independent, you constantly push beyond current thinking, never accept the status quo and reimagine new possibilities. You are not simply a dreamer but a discerning and sophisticated thinker, and you know when and where to spend your time and energy.

With your endless persistence and unbridled determination, quitting is not an option. You fully dedicate yourself to improving a product or service.

As a quick learner, you are constantly searching for ways to differentiate your product or organization in the market.

You are part artist and part scientist — and comfortable working at the intersection of both. Operating a business does not really interest you, so you are happy to delegate the mundane tasks of business management to others.

THE THREE ROLES MAKE A TEAM. Our research has found that builders have all types of profiles, and each one has its own strengths and weaknesses. Your talent profile may strongly align with a Rainmaker or a Conductor or an Expert. Or you may be a Rainmaker-Conductor or an Expert-Conductor or a Rainmaker-Expert. Though each type of alpha builder has the capability to build and grow a venture independently, the real magic happens when the three come together.

Think of these three types of alpha builders as roles on a team. If you are a Rainmaker who is focused on aggressively growing your business, you need an Expert who can dream up new products and a Conductor to manage the business. Or, if you are an Expert, find a Rainmaker and a Conductor to join you. And if you are a Conductor, round out your team with a Rainmaker and an Expert. We'll discuss the topic of forming teams later.

A NOTE ABOUT THE 10 TALENTS: The 10 builder talents do not address every factor that affects a builder's success. Non-personality variables such as skills, knowledge and experience — along with a host of external factors — play a role in determining success on your journey, and you must take them into consideration. But the 10 talents explain *who you are, what you can do and what you believe you are meant to do.* Gallup's research indicates that starting with self-awareness gives you the best chance for success.

The Builder's Method

You won't know what you can build until you know who you are. And you have to work at it constantly. Self-awareness is like a muscle — exercise strengthens it.

So let's begin the process of self-discovery — what we call "The Builder's Method."

Step ❶ Fill out your self-schema

A self-schema is your version of yourself — an internal map of your personality that you can use to understand your behavior. It is how you view yourself and the world.

When you get your BP10 report, read the detailed descriptions of your talents in **Part Three: The 10 Talents of Successful Builders**. You may think, "These make sense. I knew this about myself since I was 4 years old." Or you may be surprised, blissfully unaware of certain aspects of your personality. Whatever the case, make note of words or phrases that resonate most with you for each of your top four talents.

Here are some examples pulled from the full descriptions for Profitability and Selling:

PROFITABILITY

If you have high Profitability, ***making money*** is your primary objective.

As a builder with high Profitability, you have sharp business instincts, and you use them to price products or services to guarantee a profit on each sale. Consistent with your emphasis on money, you ***run a tight ship***, keeping a close check on operational costs. You make all decisions, big and small, with ***cost in mind*** and evaluate your decisions through the prism of profitability.

Your attitude toward data reflects your penchant for numbers. Your high Profitability talent gives you an uncanny ability to look at the same data that your managers, co-founders or employees have reviewed and come up with unique insights that they may have missed. ***Numbers are your lifeline.***

SELLING

As someone with high Selling talent, you are an ***excellent communicator*** who instinctively knows how to reach your audience. ***Incredibly persuasive***, you are a great salesperson who can influence others to accept your point of view. Your open and authentic behavior helps you forge trusting relationships with investors, customers, partners and employees that help you launch new products and services to grow your organization.

Builders with high Selling talent are ***exceptional storytellers***. You communicate the essence of your organization, your idea, or your new product or service through stories that reflect your personal experiences.

You create an emotional connection with your audience by sharing your passion and excitement about the product or service, but also by speaking to your listeners' needs.

Once you have selected the words, phrases or sentences that resonate most with you, write a self-defining characteristic — a quality that you believe is important to who you are — for each term you highlighted. Here is an example of a self-schema using Profitability and Selling talents:

Top builder talent	What resonates with me	My self-schema
Profitability	Making money	As a kid, I had a lemonade stand every summer, and even my parents had to BUY lemonade from me!
	Run a tight ship	I stick to my budget each month.
	Cost in mind	I account for every last penny I spend.
	Numbers are your lifeline	I love spreadsheets.
Selling	Excellent communicator	I adjust my message based on my audience.
	Incredibly persuasive	I get my way — always!
	Exceptional storyteller	I have a vivid imagination and a flair for storytelling.

Use the Self-Schema Tool (See Appendix) to complete your own self-schema. Write as much or as little as you like about your characteristics or behaviors that match each talent. This is not a one-time exercise. Review your self-schema often. Add to it as you observe yourself exhibiting behaviors in line with your top talents.

When you create your self-schema, your brain experiences what we call the *strengths advantage*. Focusing on what you are good at — your natural talents or your strengths — improves your performance. You think more clearly, you learn faster, your energy levels rise, you are more productive, you can work longer, and you are happier and less stressed.

Be mindful of how you use your top talents in your personal and professional life. Gallup's research shows that there are practical benefits to learning about and working in your areas of strength. We have found that when individuals and teams use their strengths, employee engagement increases by up to 15%, the enterprise's profits rise by up to 29% and sales boost by up to 19%.

Step ❷ Create a personal board of directors

Now that you have a start on your self-schema and a good understanding of your top builder talents, you are ready to form your "board of directors."

The most successful builders readily admit that they didn't get where they are by themselves. Like them, you will need support. It is important to share and get feedback from others. Who among your network of friends, coworkers, coaches and family members could be on your board? Consider people you trust, whose opinions you value, who can be honest with you, who know more than you do, and who can help with your growth and development. These are the people you want on your board.

Here are some roles to consider: coach, mentor, role model, expert, accountability partner, complementary partner and someone with shared interests. You may want as few as two or as many as 10 board members. We recommend between five and seven. Keep in mind that diversity of ideas and expertise will be beneficial in your journey as a builder.

Once you have identified your board members, determine how often you will check in with each one. Make sure to pick people who will be the most helpful to you, and stay in regular contact with them. The key to getting the maximum benefit from your personal board of directors is to have a process.

1. *How often will you interact with each board member?* You'll need regular input from some board members more than others. For instance, a coach, mentor or accountability partner is someone you will meet with regularly, say every month or every few months. But your interactions with an expert or role model may be less frequent. You are likely to consult an expert when you need focused support in a particular area, while a role model may be someone with whom you have very limited contact but consider to be an influential figure in your life.

2. *How close are you to each board member?* The type of interaction you have with each member will depend on how familiar you are with them and how well you know them. Rate your closeness level with each board member on a 5-point scale, with 1 being formal and distant and 5 being personal and close. You probably have a close relationship with a coach, mentor or friend with shared interests. You are likely to have a long history with these individuals. They will be your sounding boards, and you'll be more receptive to honest personal feedback from them.

3. *What type of support do you need?* Assembling an effective board of directors requires time and resources. To maximize each relationship and everyone's time, make a list of what you need from each board member based on their specific role. Your list should align with your immediate and long-term goals. The clearer your goals, the easier it will be for you to use each relationship to your benefit.

Here is an example of a personal board of directors for Jerome, a college senior who is interested in getting into the financial industry:

Coach	Encourages, motivates and facilitates my personal growth by helping me develop my talents

Name: Sally   **Closeness level (5-point scale):** 5 (close)

Frequency of interaction: Once every three months. Check with her about what day of the week works best. Save the dates on our calendars: March 20, June 20, September 20, December 20.

Type of support you need: Discuss my plans after college — how to get where I want to be in 5 years, 10 years. Set personal and professional goals. Hold me accountable at every step.

Mentor	Has experience and expertise in my areas of interest and aspiration

Name: Beth   **Closeness level (5-point scale):** 5 (close)

Frequency of interaction: When I need help with career-related issues.

Type of support you need: How to get a job on Wall Street.

Role model	Someone I look up to and admire for what they have achieved

Name: Warren Buffett   **Closeness level (5-point scale):** 1 (distant)

Frequency of interaction: None

Type of support you need: Learn from his life story: how he got into the world of investing and his advice to young investors. My dream is to travel to Omaha in May to meet him at the Berkshire Hathaway shareholders' meeting.

Expert	Has specific knowledge or skills that I don't have yet

Name: Alan   **Closeness level (5-point scale):** 2 (not very close)

Frequency of interaction: Once a week during the semester.

Type of support you need: Help with calculus homework. Test prep for mid-terms.

Use the Board of Directors Tool (See Appendix) to create your personal board of directors.

Step ❸ Create a purpose journal

As you begin to focus on your talents, start a journal that captures your positive experiences based on your talents, your plans for the future and the steps you will take to reach your goals.

Every time you spot a behavior in yourself or others that reflects your natural talents, write it down. Jot down three instances every day when you think, "This is something I do well naturally, and it makes me feel good." When you catalog positive experiences for a month, your brain begins to register the behaviors that align with your talent. Journaling allows your brain to relive those moments. When you write behaviors down, it signals to the brain that they matter.

Next, write down your plans for the future. What do you want to do, and how will you get there? Break your big goals into smaller goals and milestones. The more details you give, the higher the likelihood you will achieve your goals.

Write down your interactions with your board members. Connect their feedback to your goals. Keeping a record of your actions allows you to see how you make decisions and increases your self-awareness. Your journal will become a historical record that you can revisit to assess what led to your successes (or failures).

Here is Jerome's purpose journal:

Purpose Journal Tool

Top four talents

Profitability
Selling
Relationship
Determination

Positive experiences

- Could not put down the book The Intelligent Investor by Benjamin Graham
- Saved $1,000 to start my very first E-Trade account!
- Shortlisted the stocks for my portfolio
- Got an A+ on my investment paper

Plans for the future

- Short term: Summer internship in a financial firm
- Long term: Become an analyst on Wall Street

Interactions with board members

- Conversation with Sally
- She asked me to apply for summer internship at TD Ameritrade, Citibank and J.P. Morgan
- She knows someone at J.P. Morgan
- JPM application due Jan. 19
- Call Beth for the second reference letter (due Dec. 20)

Use the Purpose Journal Tool (See Appendix) to build self-awareness and to keep track of how your experiences, interactions and plans align with your talents.

Remember, building self-awareness takes discipline. You have to train your brain to identify and use your strengths. We hope this three-step process will reinforce what you already know about yourself as well as fill in some gaps. Knowing yourself is foundational to your success.

But cultivating self-awareness is just the beginning. The leap to actual building is much bigger and requires more work. It's time to take the next step toward building something.

Things to Do

1. Learn your unique mix of talents by taking the Builder Profile 10 assessment.

2. Understand the type of builder you are: Rainmaker, Conductor or Expert.

3. Fill out your self-schema to discover and direct your unique talents.

4. Form your personal board of directors. Diversity of ideas and advice will help you be a better builder.

5. Train your brain to identify and use your strengths. Keep a purpose journal for at least 30 days. Catalog your positive experiences.

THE SECOND KEY: RECOGNIZING OPPORTUNITIES

The big question facing you now is: *How do I identify opportunities to build?*

Opportunities are everywhere. Extant literature on entrepreneurial cognition and psychology indicates that an individual's likelihood of recognizing opportunities increases with:

a) prior knowledge of the environment (business, political or social)

b) motivation to change the status quo (due to improvements in a process; new developments in regulations, technology or industry; or unexpected events or demographic shifts)

c) the extent of their networks

Selecting the right idea to pursue may be the most important choice you'll make as a builder. Your ability to identify opportunities depends on how prepared you are to recognize them. First, you need to be open to recognizing opportunities in your environment. And second, you need to determine if the opportunity in front of you is the best one to pursue.

Path to Opportunity Recognition

Instead of waiting around for opportunities to show up, let's discuss a process you can use to become alert and sensitive to unexpected events, to shifts in the market or customer needs, and to the possibilities that arise from the changing conditions around you. Cultivating *builder alertness* will help you discover opportunities. The steps to becoming alert to opportunities are:

1. Start with your talents

2. Connect the dots

3. Maximize your networks

Step ❶ Start with your talents

Pay attention to what you like to do and what you don't like to do. Remember, you're likely to be more successful when you are using your natural talents because the opportunities you see and the solutions you build will be meaningful to you. To identify activities and situations that engage your talents, pay attention to these three clues: *level of engagement, accelerated learning* and *superior performance.*

a) **Level of engagement:** Have you ever been so immersed in an activity that you lose track of time? If you have, you were using your talents. Positive psychologist Mihaly Csikszentmihalyi discovered that when people are completely absorbed in an activity, they have an "optimal experience," which he calls "flow."

Talent accelerates engagement with a task or an activity. Think about your experiences with a challenging exercise, a difficult project or a new hobby when you stretched yourself to the limit to achieve something difficult but worthwhile. If you were "in the zone" — a heightened sense of alertness, effortless performance, genuine satisfaction and immense enjoyment — you were in a state of flow. When you are in a state of flow, you are using your talents.

Building something is so challenging and will require so much effort that if you don't enjoy it, it will be hard to stay interested and committed. But when you apply your talents to an opportunity, you're more likely to be good at it — and that will give you the satisfaction, inspiration and stamina you will need to stick with it.

b) **Accelerated learning:** Think about times in your life when you learned a new task, tried a new hobby or participated in an extracurricular activity. Now, think about the ones that you picked up and improved at quickly.

Talent accelerates practice and learning. When you learn an activity or task quicker than your peers do, you likely have an innate talent for it.

c) **Superior performance:** When have you naturally risen to the top? You may have noticed early success in writing or public speaking. Someone may have given you positive feedback about your musical ability or praised your performance in a sport. You might be good at organizing people or planning activities.

Talent increases performance. Look for opportunities in areas where your special abilities shine. You are more likely to achieve your goals when you are at your peak performance.

To begin the process of opportunity recognition, start an opportunity journal. At the end of each day, record all the activities and tasks you did that day. For each one, use a 5-point scale (where 1 is low and 5 is high) to rate your level of engagement with the activity, how quickly you learned or improved, and your performance.

Here is an example of Sam's opportunity journal for one day. Sam is a sophomore working her way through college.

Sam's Opportunity Journal: Day 1

Activity/Task	Engagement	Learning curve	Performance	Notes
Org chemistry lab	4	3	2	Lot of work
English lit	5	5	5	Interesting!
Band practice	5	5	5	Rocked it!
Play rehearsal	4	4	3	I need to do more research on my character
Work: TA in physiology lab	1	2	3	☹
Entrepreneurship club	5	5	NA	Heard business elevator pitches — very interesting
TA office hours	2	3	1	This stinks! I need help in chemistry!
Pre-med council meeting	5	4	3	Long road ahead!
Work out (spin cycle class)	5	5	5	Want to try something different ... maybe a tap dancing class?
Cook dinner for friends	5	5	5	Chicken spring rolls with Mediterranean-inspired mint chutney! Was a big hit!

Sam comes from a family of physicians and feels that pursuing medicine is the best career path for her. Like many students, she is busy juggling classes, work, extracurricular activities and friends, and her life moves at lightning speed. She works hard to stay focused on her goal of completing her pre-med studies with a strong enough GPA to get into a decent medical school.

After four weeks of logging entries in her opportunity journal, Sam begins to notice what's working for her and what isn't. She sees her moments of flow — being in the entrepreneurship club, writing essays for her English lit class, being on stage and cooking new dishes — as well as her performance drainers — organic chemistry and physiology lab.

She finds that she loves using the principles of chemistry when cooking new dishes, but she hates equations. She enjoys interacting with physiology students, but she thinks setting up and cleaning lab equipment is the most boring task in the world.

Sam learns that her level of engagement in an activity has a direct correlation to how much and how quickly she learns and how well she performs the activity. She has also become mindful about the parts of her routine that give her the optimal experience — total involvement and deep enjoyment.

The information Sam got from her opportunity journal led her to "accidentally" discover an opportunity. Sam realized that making dinner for friends put her "in the zone." She planned each menu carefully, combined elements from different culinary traditions and experimented using principles she had learned in her chemistry class.

Sam learned that she is at her creative best when she is cooking. Then a random comment from her friends gave her an idea. They said that they wished campus food services would serve some of Sam's creations. *What if she offered her recipes to campus dining services?* Sam has not been able to stop thinking about her idea. In the next section, we will find out what she does about it.

Log your activities every day or a few times a week, like Sam did, using the Opportunity Journal Tool (See Appendix). Keep your journal for at least four weeks to capture all your activities in a typical week. Jot down notes about your ratings. This will help you remember why you rated a particular activity as a 1 or a 5.

Pay attention to your 4 and 5 ratings, especially when you consistently give an activity a 4 or a 5 rating over several weeks. These are the activities that engage you the most — when you experience flow, learn fast and are likely to see superior performance. These activities are deeply satisfying and fulfilling to you.

As you get more involved in a particular activity, you will begin to develop a heightened sense of awareness about unmet needs, gaps, problems and issues related to that activity. Your awareness will lead to ideas that can change, improve and create new products, processes or services in that area. Select one or two ideas to focus on. These ideas will turn into opportunities as you connect the dots.

Step ❷ Connect the dots

Now that you have a good idea of what you like and don't like, start to pay attention to the events, changes and trends in your area(s) of interest that you identified in your opportunity journal. In other words, connect the dots.

Research on human cognition suggests that builders identify opportunities by making connections between seemingly unrelated events. Their ability to see patterns in disparate pieces of information and make sense of social, demographic, technological, policy or other changes happening around them leads them to ideas for new products and services.

Here is an example. Consider the events that led Charles Schwab to launch his online brokerage firm:

- a major regulatory change by the SEC
- proliferation of personal computers

- development of software that could track online transactions of goods and services
- ability to make secure financial transactions over the internet
- individual investors' frustration with high brokerage fees

How did Schwab recognize an opportunity? He was able to "connect the dots" between these seemingly unrelated events and shifts in his environment, which led to the identification of a new business opportunity.

You may ask, "What leads some people to recognize patterns and make connections between various events, while others in the same environment miss those opportunities?" Existing research on opportunity recognition suggests that an individual's ability to connect the dots depends in part on innate talent (e.g., creativity, optimism, perception of risk) and to a large extent on prior knowledge and life or work experiences.

Schwab had many years of experience in the financial industry. His vast knowledge of the field helped him see how new technological developments "connected" to changes in regulation and to customers' changing expectations. His experiences, knowledge and talent put him in a unique position to recognize the opportunity at hand. Another person might have worked in the same industry but may have had different experiences, different knowledge sets and different talents and so would have been less likely to connect the same dots.

Stephanie Breedlove's experience of launching her business is an excellent real-life case study of how builders identify new business opportunities, launch new ventures and grow highly successful businesses. Her story and others in this book bring our builder principles to life. These builders' journeys can help you understand the context of a problem, identify solutions and figure out how to apply those solutions to real-world situations.

In her book, *All In: How Women Entrepreneurs Can Think Bigger, Build Sustainable Businesses, and Change the World*, Breedlove describes how she recognized a need in the market that led her and her husband to launch a new business.

When Stephanie Breedlove and her husband hired their nanny, they decided to enter into a formal employer-employee arrangement with her. Becoming an employer meant that they would have to withhold taxes; pay an employer tax; and provide healthcare, paid vacation days and sick days — things that neither Breedlove nor her husband knew anything about.

As they made their way through the process, they realized that there might be other families who could benefit from what they had learned. There was no one offering these services in the market. So they launched Breedlove & Associates (now known as HomePay) — a company that helped families pay their in-home caregivers legally, offering payroll processing, tax remittance and HR services.

Breedlove had identified a market gap after observing and experiencing these trends:

- proliferation of dual-income families that need in-home childcare services
- increasing population of in-home caregivers (nannies, health aides, housekeepers)
- the Breedloves' desire to pay their nanny legally

The combined education, skills, and life and work experiences of Breedlove and her husband enabled them to connect the dots, which led to a new and profitable business opportunity.

You may be thinking that "connecting the dots" is all well and good for those who have extensive work experience, education and expertise, but what about novice builders? How do they connect seemingly disparate events and information? Let's see what happened with Sam's idea. Here are the circumstances that led Sam to recognize an opportunity:

- dining services across campus offer non-descript and boring food
- a large segment of students living in residence halls are open to diverse food experiences
- Sam loves designing new dishes

Sam connected the dots between her observations by starting with her talents (her creativity in coming up with new dishes) and then paying attention to her environment. She used her knowledge of the food choices available on campus, her experience of dining with her friends and the feedback she received from her network about the new dishes to see the possibilities.

Her idea took shape: Every week, she would provide campus dining services with unique recipes that can be prepared in less than 30 minutes with easily available ingredients. Sam would train the dining services staff each week to prepare the food items. She thinks that offering once-a-week surprise entrees on the menu will boost student loyalty and retention.

Sam has an idea, but she needs to do a lot more work to shape it into a viable opportunity. She is a novice builder with no background, formal training or experience in culinary design. So, she has to focus her efforts on gathering as much information as she can about the trends and changes in college dining service operations, food technology, the nutritional value of her recipes, the expectations of the customers (students), and the university's policies concerning food safety. Gathering information will give Sam, a rookie builder, a definite edge in identifying feasible opportunities.

Once you have narrowed down the idea(s) that emerge from your opportunity journal, pay attention to the trends, events and changes relevant to your idea — issues, problems and gaps between *what is* and *what should be*. Be as specific as you can in your journal entries. The greater the specificity of your notes, the clearer the links between seemingly unrelated events and changes will be.

Step ❸ Maximize your networks

The next step in the opportunity recognition process is to talk to people in your social circle, especially those who are working in or are knowledgeable about your area of interest. Start with your board members. They are invested in your success and your future. Use them as a sounding board for your ideas.

Consult the expert and the role model on your board. Your role model may be someone you don't know personally but who is well-versed in your area of interest and a source of inspiration for you. Read about this person's experience in the early stages of the building process.

It is also a good time to touch base with your mentor and coach. Get their feedback. They might introduce you to others in the field, give you advice, offer alternatives or identify resources you will need to turn your idea into reality. To make the best use of everyone's time, make a list of questions to ask each board member.

Sam got critical help from her network. Her undergraduate adviser introduced her to the director of dining services via email. This opened the door for an introductory meeting. Her adviser also suggested that Sam create a "freemium model" — free recipes for the first five weeks, followed by a per-plate fee after that.

Her mentor introduced her to a Ph.D. student in nutrition science who is helping her assess the calorie and fat content of each entree. Sam hopes that doing her homework will strengthen her pitch to the director of dining services. Sam also decided to take a class in nutrition science. This will serve two purposes: She will get credit for the course, and she will be working on her idea as a class project. One of Sam's friends suggested letting students rate her entrees. The customer satisfaction data Sam collects will become a critical part of her pitch to continue her services.

Sharing her idea and seeking feedback from her board members gave Sam more information and learning, a broader social network, and access to additional resources to refine her idea. Just like Sam, the wider your network is and the more you interact with others, the higher your likelihood of recognizing potentially valuable opportunities will be.

Assessing Opportunities

Now that you are beginning to think like a builder, it is time to vet your ideas. Determining whether an opportunity is practical and worth pursuing is a critical part of the opportunity recognition process. You may start with one idea and continue to iterate on it until a final product or service emerges, or you may have multiple ideas that you can process simultaneously.

Vetting your idea(s) might lead you in new and different directions than you originally anticipated. Rarely do builders start with a fully developed idea or know what their venture will ultimately look like.

Opportunity recognition is an ongoing process. Be prepared to continuously refine and develop your ideas and fill your knowledge gaps as you adapt and adjust your goals. Be open to the process of exploration.

To get started, ask yourself:

- Why are you doing this? **(Purpose)**
- What are you building? **(Product/Service)**
- Who are your customers, and how are you helping them? **(Customer needs)**
- What differentiates your product/service from others in the market? **(Value add)**
- What financial and social resources and skill sets do you bring to the table? **(Resources)**
- How much are you willing to risk/lose to make your idea a reality? **(Affordable loss)**

    Saras Sarasvathy, a leading scholar of entrepreneurship at the University of Virginia, defines the *affordable-loss principle* as a determination of how much one [a builder] is willing to lose in order to start a venture.

- What does success look like? **(Success)**

Here is Sam's initial assessment of her opportunity to offer healthy and global flavors to the resident students on her college campus:

- **Purpose:** Create a culture and community around authentic and varied food offerings.
- **Product/Service:** Two new recipes for food services every week. Consult with and train the staff.
- **Customer needs:** Her customers are students in her generation on her campus. They expect healthful, fresh and adventurous flavors. Campus food service professionals are not meeting these needs.
- **Value add:** a) Sam offers a variety of dishes at a fraction of the cost of hiring trained culinarians, certified master chefs or visiting celebrity chefs; b) Having a student involved in cooking and food production makes food services more accessible to students and fosters loyalty.
- **Resources:** a) Her network provides advice, support and resources; b) Her time, energy and commitment; c) Experience cooking for her friends.
- **Affordable loss:** Sam is psychologically committed to seeing this project through and is giving herself one semester to make it happen. She decided to take the plunge after telling herself, "I have no money to invest, but I will spend all my energy and time making this work. I will give myself one semester. Worst case scenario, none of this will work, and I will start next semester with a whole lot of learning."
- **Success:** a) Sam will charge $25 per recipe plus one hour of consulting for the first five weeks of the semester ($25 x 2 recipes per week x 5 weeks = $250). For the next 11 weeks of the semester, she will charge $40 per recipe and consulting ($40 x 2 recipes per week x 11 weeks = $880). Plus, she will charge $1 per plate sold throughout the semester. So a successful semester would be $1,130 ($250 + $880) + $1 per plate; b) 10% growth in customers every semester.

Take a look at Sam's storyboard, where she sketches out multiple paths to her goals.

Sam's Storyboard

	Idea 1	Idea 2
Opportunity	Offer healthy and global flavors to resident students.	Start a wellness center after medical school; explore link between food and health.
Purpose	Create a culture and community around authentic and varied food offerings.	Pursue a degree in culinary medicine — medical students learn to cook and provide nutritional advice to patients.
Product/ Service	Phase 1: a) Share two new recipes with campus food services every week. b) Consult with and train the staff. Phase 2: Students pick fresh ingredients; prepare food in front of students.	Nutritional advice to patients.
Customer needs	Phase 1: Students expect healthy, fresh and adventurous flavors. Campus food service professionals are not meeting these needs. Phase 2: Create memorable experiences for students.	Patients expect education about food and nutrition to prevent diseases.
Value add	a) Variety at a fraction of the cost. b) Entrees created "for the student by the student" results in better accessibility and fosters loyalty.	A physician with culinary training.
Resources	a) Network for advice, support and resources. b) Time, energy and commitment. c) Experience cooking for friends.	a) Work for two years in a wellness center that focuses on nutrition. b) Build up savings. c) Create a wider network.
Affordable loss	No money to invest, but I will spend energy and time making this work. I will give myself one semester. Worst case, lesson learned.	a) $75,000 in savings. b) One year of my time; if I fail, get a job as a physician.
Success	Phase 1: a) $1,130 + $1 per plate sold. b) 10% growth in number of customers every semester. Phase 2: a) $5,000 per semester. b) Growth in number of customers.	Profitable wellness center.

As you can see from Sam's storyboard, she does not have a specific predetermined goal. She will allow her goals to emerge through an iterative process. First, she will try Idea 1. If food services accepts her recipes and training (Phase 1), she may try a variation of the original idea by adding a new component — offering on-the-spot cooked meals to students (Phase 2).

It is possible that both options will be a hit with customers. If so, Sam might add services, for instance, food delivery to off-campus students. On the other hand, it is possible that neither options in Idea 1 will materialize into anything of substance. In that case, she will learn from her experience and pursue Idea 2: Train as a physician with an expertise in culinary science.

Sam defines success in economic terms and business-related factors — revenue, growth in customer base and profit. Research indicates that highly experienced builders clearly focus on factors that make a business successful such as cash flow, profit or revenue. If you plan to build in the nonprofit or community sector, we still recommend that you focus on business metrics. Even if profit maximization is not the objective, you still need to ensure that you do not have a loss. Concentrate on factors such as funds generation, budget management, cost reduction and social return on investment (impact on your customers/community).

Use the Storyboard Tool (See Appendix) to assess your opportunities. As you evaluate the feasibility and potential economic value of your ideas, you will begin to see a viable path forward. In the next section, we will discuss developing your ideas into ventures.

Things to Do

1. Start with your talents. Identify the activities that engage you most — when you learn fastest and perform with excellence. Focus on one or two areas of interest from your opportunity journal.

2. Connect the dots. Learn to recognize patterns by paying attention to events, changes and trends in your area(s) of interest. Articulate your ideas in the notes section of your opportunity journal.

3. Maximize your networks. Talk to people in your social circle, and use feedback from your board members to refine your ideas and access resources so you can turn your dreams into reality.

4. Assess your opportunities. Create a storyboard with multiple paths to get to your goal(s).

THE THIRD KEY: ACTIVATING ON IDEAS

Action matters more than ideas. Your future depends on your actions. Activating on your ideas is where talent and opportunity meet hard work to build successful products and ventures.

Great builders begin by developing a basic version of their product or service — a minimally viable product (MVP). Then, they put their MVP in front of early adopters (i.e., customers). They learn from customer feedback and repeat and refine until their product meets customer expectations, thus increasing the chances of their venture's survival and success.

Using the ideas you generated from the opportunity recognition exercise, you will learn how to turn your ideas into hypotheses (Who are my customers? Do they need what I am building? Will they pay for it?), launch experiments to test each hypothesis, learn from each experiment, refine your product or service based on what you learned, and test again until you have a profitable and scalable business model. By following this cycle of *hypothesize, experiment, measure outcomes, learn, hypothesize again*, you will be able to build a sustainable and repeatable business model that brings in paying customers.

Generating Hypotheses

A builder's path to success is paved with challenges, setbacks and hardships. As a builder, you will encounter uncertainty, risk and doubt.

The best way to reduce risk is to start small. Successful builders do not engage in impulsive or uninformed risk-taking. They evaluate opportunities thoroughly and minimize risk by taking small incremental steps. They begin with certain assumptions, which we'll call hypotheses.

Let's take a look at the assumptions Stephanie Breedlove made when she had the idea of starting a company to help families pay their in-home caregivers legally.

Stephanie Breedlove's Activation Chart: Hypotheses

Hypotheses	Experiments	Outcomes	The future
H1: Relationship-based marketing and sales is the best customer-acquisition strategy.			
H2: Families who hire in-home caregivers want to pay them legally.			
H3: Customers will pay for a high-touch service in payroll, tax and labor law.			
H4: Unlimited phone consultation as part of the standard service will increase customer loyalty and lengthen the customer relationship.			

Breedlove started with some basic research into payroll and labor law. Remember, she had no experience in this field. She created a website and some basic marketing materials, defined her offering (client education materials and deliverables) and who she was offering it to (target customer), and outlined the process of delivering her service to her customers. And she did this all on a shoestring budget while she was employed full time for a consulting firm.

An MVP — a bare bones, no frills product or service that is cobbled together with minimal resources — was born.

The purpose of an MVP is to prove that your idea is viable and that there are customers willing to embrace it. A simple website with some marketing and educational materials was enough for Breedlove to launch an experiment and test her hypotheses.

Sam used her storyboard to form her hypotheses. Here are the assumptions she made:

Sam's Activation Chart: Hypotheses

Hypotheses	Experiments	Outcomes	The future
H1: Campus dining services will be open to carrying my dishes.			
H2: College students are hungry for healthy, fresh and adventurous food on campus.			
H3: Students are willing to pay extra for healthy, global flavors.			
H4: Having a student involved in food production makes food services more accessible to students and boosts loyalty and retention.			

Sam started by working on her recipes. She consulted a nutritional science student to estimate the caloric and fat content of each recipe. Next, she came up with a unique marketing strategy: She wrote a "recipe" article about a no-heat Peruvian dessert to stimulate interest in her dishes. Her plan was to publish the article in the college newspaper the week of the launch and invite readers to "armchair travel" to Peru to test the recipe.

This is a low-cost but highly effective marketing technique called "content marketing," which focuses on creating content via an article, blog, video or social media post to attract customers. At the end of her article, Sam asked students to enter their names into a drawing for one of 15 free lunch coupons at the dining hall.

Sam also created and posted flyers on several bulletin boards around campus, and she recruited a few friends to distribute the flyers the week of her launch.

Her MVP was ready. Several hours of planning and work, three friends, and $115 ($10 for photocopying flyers and $105 for 15 lunch coupons at $7 each) is all it took to develop her MVP. She was ready to pitch her idea to the director of campus dining.

Use the Activation Chart Tool (See Appendix) to begin forming your hypotheses. Go back to your storyboard and review what you wrote down for "Opportunity," "Purpose," "Product/Service" and "Customer needs." Ask yourself, "What am I trying to provide to the market? Are there customers who care about it? How do I reach my customers? Would they pay for the product/service?" Answers to these questions will help you build your hypotheses.

Once you have formulated your hypotheses, test them empirically, collect feedback from your customers and refine your business concept.

Launching Experiments

To confirm or disprove your hypotheses, you will have to launch a few experiments. You need to validate every part of your plan with customers. Remember, the only thing you need is a customer.

This bears repeating: *Look for customers, not funding.* Customers are the cash flow you need to sustain and grow your venture.

You might ask yourself these questions about two big unknowns when you are building something new: "How do I find my first customer?" and "How do I figure out what the customer needs?"

How do I find my first customer?

The answer to your first question — *How do I find my first customer?* — is threefold:

1. Go back to asking yourself who you are, what your beliefs and values are, and who you see using your product or service. For example, Sam could see students like her, who lived on campus and wanted better meal options, as her target customers — even though she could have sold her recipes through other channels such as marketing to local restaurants or creating videos on YouTube. But she decided to sell to students because that is what she believes in — helping other students enjoy healthy and tasty food choices.

2. Another way to find your first customer is by using your work experience or any experience you have had with a similar product. Sam had shared her dishes with her friends. She knew they enjoyed her cooking. So making students her first customers was the natural outcome of her direct experience with her peers. Stephanie Breedlove used her own struggles with paying her nanny legally to find her first set of customers — other families in a similar situation.

3. Finally, ask yourself, "Who would be interested in trying my product or service?" A professor, a peer, a friend, anyone on your personal board of directors or someone in your network — can any of these people be your first customer? Consider your initial

customer to be your strategic partner. Cultivate a relationship of trust by staying in close touch with this person. Research indicates that repeated interactions with your initial customer lead to an improved product, critical market information, and new ideas for products or services.

How do I figure out what the customer needs?

The only way to figure out what your customer needs is to go out and sell to your potential customers.

Highly successful builders do not waste time and resources developing their product or service to perfection, nor do they spend money on market research or other marketing activities. They go out and start selling. They find potential customers before the product is ready. Their market research is the face-to-face interaction with their customers. They listen to their customers and learn from their behavior — how customers buy the product or service, which features they like and which they don't, and what is important and what is irrelevant to them.

Empirical evidence you obtain from the customer becomes the basis for refining and improving your early-stage product or service, identifying additional markets, or pivoting to a new direction. Use customer behavior to confirm or disprove your hypotheses.

Here are the steps Stephanie Breedlove took to test her hypotheses. Breedlove strongly believed that in-home caregivers deserve to be treated professionally, with a regular paycheck, benefits and retirement savings. So first, she contacted in-home-care placement agencies and offered to educate them about their legal obligation to the in-home-care service providers.

Then she offered to provide free phone consulting to the placement centers' clients (families who hired the caregivers) with the hope that her high-touch customer strategy would lead to client referrals. Her "test" continued for two years while she was employed full time (low-risk strategy). The results were positive. She confirmed hypotheses 1 and 2:

- ✓ H1: Relationship-based marketing and sales is the best customer-acquisition strategy.

- ✓ H2: Families who hire in-home caregivers want to pay them legally.

Energized by the positive feedback, Breedlove took the plunge into building and growing her venture full time. Her high-touch phone consultation strategy was yielding high returns. She decided to expand her offerings by adding a new fully automated self-service component, while constantly improving the quality of her product. She also gradually added new products like health insurance and workers' compensation to her portfolio of services, thus increasing her value proposition to her clients (families).

Breedlove also expanded her customer base. She started by offering HR and payroll services to families who hire nannies (her initial customer segment) and then expanded her customer base to include all families who have any type of in-home employment relationship. This is how she grew her customer base from 10 families to 100 to 1,000 to 10,000 and finally to 100,000 families (customers). She had confirmed hypotheses 3 and 4:

- ✓ H3: Customers will pay for a high-touch service in payroll, tax and labor law.

- ✓ H4: Unlimited phone consultation as part of the standard service will increase customer loyalty and lengthen the customer relationship.

Stephanie Breedlove's Activation Chart: Experiments

Hypotheses	Experiments	Outcomes	The future
H1: Relationship-based marketing and sales is the best customer-acquisition strategy.	Educate in-home-care placement agencies about their legal obligation to in-home service providers		
H2: Families who hire in-home caregivers want to pay them legally.	Offer free phone consulting to families		
H3: Customers will pay for a high-touch service in payroll, tax and labor law.	Add fully automated self-service and new products (health insurance and workers' comp)		
H4: Unlimited phone consultation as part of the standard service will increase customer loyalty and lengthen the customer relationship.	Offer unlimited phone consultation to families		

Note how Breedlove moved from a few customers to a broader market of families with various types of in-home-care needs. She selected her initial customers (families who hire nannies) and marketing channel (placement services) through her own experience hiring nannies. Having identified a target customer segment, she grew her customer base by:

a) developing new products (fully automated self-service component, health insurance and workers' compensation)

b) broadening her service to accommodate any household that requires in-home employees, such as senior care providers, household staff, personal assistants and estate managers

Sam met with the food services director and explained her idea and the rollout plan to launch her experiment with customers. The director agreed to run a limited trial in one of the central dining halls on campus. Hypothesis 1 confirmed:

✓ H1: Campus dining services will be open to carrying my dishes.

Every day, about 450-500 students eat in or take out lunch from the dining hall where Sam's first dish was served. Sam's dish was included in a large food station with 20 other entrees.

Sam was there to watch how the customers (students) behaved. She noticed that about one-third of the students (165 of the 500) were curious about her dish, but only about 10% who stopped to look (16 of the 165) bought the dish. Three percent conversion rate on day one was not a bad start (16/500 x 100 = 3.2%). *Conversion rate* is the percentage of traffic that completes a purchase transaction. Sam was encouraged.

She continued to gather more evidence. In week two of her experiment, she learned that most students prefer a quick take-out meal instead of a sit-down meal. Armed with the data, Sam met with the director of food services and proposed setting up a split-test. A *split-test* compares two versions of a product or service to see which one performs better with customers. Here are the two versions Sam tested:

- Version 1: A stand-alone station inside the dining hall to differentiate her product from the 20 other food items
- Version 2: A to-go station just outside the dining hall

Over the next two weeks, customers split between the two versions of Sam's product. She was back to measuring customer behavior. The numbers were up. Overall conversion rate climbed to 30%. Hypothesis 2 was confirmed:

✓ H2: College students are hungry for healthy, fresh and adventurous food on campus.

The station inside the dining hall was more popular than the to-go station. Sam talked to a few students and found that they were not willing to pay extra at the to-go station. Dining services charged a small fee for the to-go station. So, Sam could not confirm Hypothesis 3:

✓ H3: Students are willing to pay extra for healthy, global flavors.

Sam did not yet have the data to prove Hypothesis 4:

✓ H4: Having a student involved in food production makes food services more accessible to students and boosts loyalty and retention.

Sam's Activation Chart: Experiments

Hypotheses	Experiments	Outcomes	The future
H1: Campus dining services will be open to carrying my dishes.	Pitched MVP to dining services		
H2: College students are hungry for healthy, fresh and adventurous food on campus.	Marketing: recipe article Word-of-mouth marketing Week 1-2: Launched two dishes Week 3: Started a stand-alone station and a to-go station		
H3: Students are willing to pay extra for healthy, global flavors.	Week 3: to-go station		
H4: Having a student involved in food production makes food services more accessible to students and boosts loyalty and retention.	Consult and train dining services staff		

You can see how Sam's experiments with real customers yielded an amazing amount of information. What delivery method works best with busy students? How much are they willing to pay? Sam learned all this in less than five weeks using a *zero-resources-to-market* strategy. Saras Sarasvathy explains the zero-resources-to-market principle as a creative way for builders to bring their products to market with minimal cost.

Based on what she learned, Sam is making improvements and enhancements to her current services as well as thinking about new ideas. She is just getting started.

This iterative approach of building hypotheses followed by experiments with real customers followed by more hypotheses and still more experiments will inform Sam how to build a product that fulfills her vision of providing healthy, flavorful foods while meeting her customers' needs. By the time her finished product is ready, she will have an established set of customers who rely on her product to solve their food problem on the college campus.

Like Sam, you can run your own experiments. Offer the initial version of your product or service to your early adopters. Then pay attention to their behaviors and comments. Your first customers will give you critical feedback that will improve your product or service.

Use the Activation Chart Tool (See Appendix) to make notes on your experiments and what you learn from them. Your notes will become the historical record of your decision-making process, which you can review to see what worked and what didn't. This will help you become a better builder.

Measuring Outcomes

A key component of your activation process is having measurable and concrete business outcomes to gauge the success (or failure) of your experiments. These metrics evaluate the overall health of your MVP and confirm that you have a reasonably good grasp of the following:

- I understand customers' problems or the need in the market.
- Customers find my product or service valuable (value hypothesis).
- A large number of customers are interested in my product or service (growth hypothesis).
- I can make a profit with what my customers are willing to pay for my product or service.

Let's look at the results of Stephanie Breedlove's experiments. Breedlove's core marketing strategy was to cultivate relationships with placement firms and reach her customers (families) through them. She trained, consulted and built connections with more than 125 placement firms in the first two years of her business. This resulted in loyal exclusive partnerships with more than 100 of these firms. The relationships she established led to significant growth in subsequent years.

Next, her offer of high-touch, unlimited phone consultation yielded high returns. More than 50% of on-the-phone sales consultations resulted in a client. Customers stayed with the company twice as long compared with any other competitor. In other words, the placement firms and families found Breedlove's product valuable. She validated her value hypothesis.

Her customer base grew from 10 to 100,000 families. And revenue kept pace, starting with $3,000 in year one, $17,000 in year two (Breedlove was employed full time for the first two years), $26,000 in year three (first year as a full-time builder), $725,000 five years later, $6 million in five more years and $15 million in another five years.

Breedlove's growth trajectory in the early years of her business validated her growth hypothesis. There are a large number of customers interested in her product, and customers are willing to pay for her product, which results in a profitable venture. Breedlove had clearly tapped into a market need.

Stephanie Breedlove's Activation Chart: Outcomes

Hypotheses	Experiments	Outcomes	The future
H1: Relationship-based marketing and sales is the best customer-acquisition strategy.	Educate in-home-care placement agencies about their legal obligation to in-home service providers	Exclusive partnership with 100 placement firms by year 2	
H2: Families who hire in-home caregivers want to pay them legally.	Offer free phone consulting to families	Customer base grew rapidly	
H3: Customers will pay for a high-touch service in payroll, tax and labor law.	Add fully automated self-service and new products (health insurance and workers' comp)	50% conversion rate Revenue growth	
H4: Unlimited phone consultation as part of the standard service will increase customer loyalty and lengthen the customer relationship.	Offer unlimited phone consultation to families	Clients stayed with company twice as long	

Sam is only a few weeks into her initial experiment, but she has clear, quantifiable outcomes. In the first week, 3% of students bought her product. When she talked with potential customers, they showed interest in her product and found it valuable. She is on her way to validating her value hypothesis.

Setting up a separate station for her dishes inside the dining hall and adding a to-go station outside moved the numbers up to 30%. This shows that new customers are discovering her product and that there is real growth potential.

Sam's Activation Chart: Outcomes

Hypotheses	Experiments	Outcomes	The future
H1: Campus dining services will be open to carrying my dishes.	Pitched MVP to dining services	Project accepted	
H2: College students are hungry for healthy, fresh and adventurous food on campus.	Marketing: recipe article	Moderately successful	
	Word-of-mouth marketing	Moderately successful	
	Week 1-2: Launched two dishes	Week 1-2: 3.2% conversion rate	
	Week 3: Started a stand-alone station and a to-go station	Week 3: Stand-alone station conversion rate climbed to 30%	
H3: Students are willing to pay extra for healthy, global flavors.	Week 3: to-go station	Lower adoption rate; won't pay extra	
H4: Having a student involved in food production makes food services more accessible to students and boosts loyalty and retention.	Consult and train dining services staff	Too soon to tell	

Sam has more experiments to conduct. For example, she has yet to work out her delivery channels. Sam is in the early stages of building a venture, and the results from her experiments will guide her journey. Perhaps the meals-on-the-go idea will take off. And if it doesn't, then she may pivot to delivering farm-to-table food to her customers. Or if her customers are interested in learning about new cultures, she may become a nutritional consultant-cum-cultural guide and offer her customers the experience of other cultures through her food, writing or lectures.

The process of building something may take you in different directions than you originally imagined. You may start with a general goal — an idea of what you want to build (product or service) for whom (customer) and how (your business model to deliver your product to the customer). But the experiments you conduct and the results from your experiments will likely alter your plans, push you to adapt your strategy or point you in a new direction. With each experiment or iteration, you will get closer to building a product or service that a customer actually wants to buy (finding the product/market fit).

Confirming your value proposition to customers is a critical step for a sustainable venture. Once you have validated your hypotheses with early customers, decide if it is time to take your product to a wider market or if you need to keep fine-tuning.

Dream Big

If you are ready to roll out your product or service to a broader market, you have reached an important milestone. You have validated your value and growth hypotheses. You have figured out who your customers are, what you are offering them and how you will deliver your product or service.

With your business model validated, you are on your way to building a sustainable venture. As you continue to build, don't forget to dream big. It is important to think about growth and scale.

For Stephanie Breedlove, it was time to think about expanding her customer base to become a leader in professionalizing the in-home-care industry.

Stephanie Breedlove's Activation Chart: The Future

Hypotheses	Experiments	Outcomes	The future
H1: Relationship-based marketing and sales is the best customer-acquisition strategy.	Educate in-home-care placement agencies about their legal obligation to in-home service providers	Exclusive partnership with 100 placement firms by year 2	Grow nationally Become a leader in professionalizing in-home-care industry
H2: Families who hire in-home caregivers want to pay them legally.	Offer free phone consulting to families	Customer base grew rapidly	
H3: Customers will pay for a high-touch service in payroll, tax and labor law.	Add fully automated self-service and new products (health insurance and workers' comp)	50% conversion rate Revenue growth	
H4: Unlimited phone consultation as part of the standard service will increase customer loyalty and lengthen the customer relationship.	Offer unlimited phone consultation to families	Clients stayed with company twice as long	

Sam has future goals as well — maybe offering new ways to deliver her dishes or even a national wellness center.

Sam's Activation Chart: The Future

Hypotheses	Experiments	Outcomes	The future
H1: Campus dining services will be open to carrying my dishes.	Pitched MVP to dining services	Project accepted	Mobile meals
H2: College students are hungry for healthy, fresh and adventurous food on campus.	Marketing: recipe article	Moderately successful	Take & bake
	Word-of-mouth marketing	Moderately successful	National wellness centers
	Week 1-2: Launched two dishes	Week 1-2: 3.2% conversion rate	
	Week 3: Started a stand-alone station and a to-go station	Week 3: Stand-alone station conversion rate climbed to 30%	
H3: Students are willing to pay extra for healthy, global flavors.	Week 3: to-go station	Lower adoption rate; won't pay extra	
H4: Having a student involved in food production makes food services more accessible to students and boosts loyalty and retention.	Consult and train dining services staff	Too soon to tell	

Set aside time to think about what could be. Jot down your ideas in "The future" section of your activation chart. On days when you spend 100% of your time just managing the day-to-day functions of your venture, these ideas will be your reminders of what is possible.

The next step toward growth is building a team. A great team is critical and can accelerate the growth phase.

Things to Do

1. Start by generating hypotheses. Go back to your storyboard and ask yourself, "What am I trying to provide? Are there potential customers who care about my product or service? How do I reach my customers?" Answers to these questions will lead you to build your hypotheses.

2. Launch a few experiments to test your hypotheses. Find your early adopters, and figure out what they need. Based on their feedback, make changes to your product or service. Then build a new set of hypotheses, and test again. Repeat until you have a product or service that customers actually want to buy.

3. Measure outcomes. Measurable and concrete business outcomes will help you prove or disprove your hypotheses.

4. Dream big. Take time to think about what is possible. Think about growth and scale.

THE FOURTH KEY: BUILDING A TEAM

Now that you have a good understanding of your customers and their needs, it is time to build your team.

The romanticized image of a lone builder — who, through a combination of imagination, grit and some luck, becomes successful — is out of touch with reality. Turning an idea into a product or service requires a web of both direct ties — family, colleagues and friends — and indirect ties — extended networks of investors, suppliers, mentors, employees and the larger community. The connections in a builder's network not only bring new resources to the venture, but also diversity of opinions and perspectives based on who they are, their background and their knowledge base.

The involvement and commitment of each member in your network can shape your initial product or service, open new markets, broaden your network, and improve your venture's ability to survive contingencies and shocks. So it's not surprising that many studies have found that ventures started and managed by teams are more sustainable and successful than those with solo founders.

Using a talent-based perspective, we will explore how to create a well-rounded leadership team that includes a Rainmaker, a Conductor and an Expert. We will also discuss strategies for how to build an extended team — a network that includes various stakeholders and partners who are invested in your success.

Building Your Leadership Team

The people side of your venture is more important than your product, strategy or funding.

The problem is that too often, builders select co-founders and early partners from their immediate network of family, friends and coworkers. Linking up with others who are similar to you results in team members who are similar in skills; educational background; work experience; and demographic characteristics such as age, gender, race and ethnicity.

Working with people who are just like you *does* reduce the likelihood of conflict, creates social and emotional support, and makes it easier to access much-needed resources for the early-stage venture.

But homogenous teams also limit a builder's world by restricting access to diverse resources — human and financial — and new information, both of which are critical for growth. As much as homogeneity has its benefits, functional diversity (different competencies or work experiences) and cognitive diversity (different ways of thinking or tackling problems) on a team are essential for growth.

Let's look at an example of an existing team from an early-stage venture. Amrita, along with her coworkers, Jordan and Blanca, founded a software company called QuantumPro a few years ago. They develop software related to business intelligence in the financial sector.

Like many young businesses, the company lacks clear roles and titles, with each member of the team doing whatever needs to be done on a day-to-day basis. Blanca, the programmer extraordinaire, manages all things technical. Amrita and Jordan, the super-smart go-getter generalists, alternate between business development, sales, product and finance — juggling their responsibilities depending on the day.

QuantumPro recently won its first million-dollar commitment from an investor — a sign that they were finally getting some traction in the market. Besides giving them money, the investor, an influential figure in the financial industry, brought along tons of contacts and advice. But having an investor on board has also made life more complicated for this tiny startup.

They now have to set up a board of directors made up of the investor, the three founders and one external person acceptable to both parties. The board will have ultimate power over all decisions related to the business. The company is also considering hiring its first employee to handle the increased volume of new prospect inquiries and sales.

The investor is pushing the team to have a clear organizational structure with well-defined job functions. It is time to clarify roles.

All three co-founders took Gallup's BP10 assessment to better understand the talent distribution on their team, determine the best role for each person, and identify blind spots and gaps in their team talent profile.

QuantumPro's Team Talent Profile

Name	Amrita	Jordan	Blanca
Role	Rainmaker	Rainmaker	Expert
Top four talents	Confidence	Profitability	Determination
	Selling	Confidence	Delegator
	Determination	Selling	Disruptor
	Risk	Determination	Relationship

The QuantumPro team is well-equipped with two Rainmakers (Characteristics: self-confident, focused on profitability, persuasive, forward-thinking, intensely driven, high sales talent, high relationship talent and optimistic perception of risk) and one Expert (Characteristics: creative, independent, persistent, determined, reimagines new possibilities, thinker and learner) but lacks a Conductor (Characteristics: delegator, team builder, self-assured, energetic, driven, fixated on growth and hardworking). A deeper look at the team talent map provides a clear picture of some of the interpersonal dynamics among the three co-founders.

Team Talent Map for QuantumPro

Name	Amrita	Jordan	Blanca
Role	Rainmaker	Rainmaker	Expert
Top four talents	Confidence Selling Determination Risk	Profitability Confidence Selling Determination	Determination Delegator Disruptor Relationship

What insights did you get from seeing your collective talents on the team talent map?

Our team talent map explains why we have survived five years without any external funding. Blanca creates what customers need, and the two of us as Rainmakers find customers. Together, we have kept the company afloat.

What are the team's areas of greatest strength?

Selling is our greatest strength. We are good at it.

What are the team's potential gaps?

Though good at product development and sales, we are not positioned well for growth. None of us has time or talent to put processes in place, build a team, set goals and hold others accountable for them. We need a Conductor.

Is there a business problem you are trying to solve? How will you use your team's strengths to reach a solution?

Since receiving external funding, we are required to put together a board. Looking at our talent map, we need to add a board member who has a strong network in the financial industry. We need someone who can be an advocate for our product and company.

Whom else do you need on your team?

We also need to hire our first employee. We are looking for someone who has Disruptor and Knowledge in their top four talents. We need a strong, creative programmer to work with Blanca.

Amrita and Jordan have considerable overlap in their top four talents; both of them have dominant Confidence, Selling and Determination talents. They're both hard-charging salespeople with immense confidence, persuasive communication skills and tenacious perseverance. While Amrita doesn't have Jordan's eye for profitability, she makes up for it with her ability to manage risks. And what Jordan lacks in an optimistic perception of risk, he makes up for with an intense focus on profitability.

So far, so good with the team's dynamics. They all work well together playing off each other's strengths, with a thread of strong determination running through the team.

Amrita is the one who came up with the idea to start the company and recruited the others, and she is the firm's majority shareholder. She sees herself as the Rainmaker who loves being the voice and face of her company. A big-picture thinker with a focus on the long term, she is the top contender for the role of CEO.

Blanca is clearly the Expert. She is the genius coder completely focused on building the technology that will drive the business forward. She has very little to do with the day-to-day management of the business.

With Amrita already fulfilling the Rainmaker role, this leaves Jordan without a clear role on the team. Some would see this situation as a big plus: two highly talented Rainmakers pursuing revenue growth and profitability — a strategy that has been beneficial for the early-stage venture.

However, Gallup advised the QuantumPro team to clearly identify the chain of command and to divide decision-making and responsibilities between Amrita and Jordan to avoid future complications. Recognizing the strengths and expertise of each, Gallup suggested that Jordan may want to focus more on the financial, legal and product decision-making (decisions regarding the product, price, promotion and distribution channels), while Amrita takes a more outward-facing role of fundraising, sales and positioning the company in the market.

The team talent map also exposes the gaps or blind spots in this team's talent. For instance, the team has no one in the role of Conductor, which is critical for growth and scale. When asked about this, both Amrita and Jordan readily admitted that they have zero interest in the mundane tasks of running the business. Both would rather be chasing customers than dealing with the day-to-day management of the business. In fact, Amrita very dramatically said, "I'd rather kill myself than do things like paperwork or hire staff or figure out how to systematize some process."

The team's collectively high Determination is probably keeping the company afloat for now, but they desperately need a Conductor if they want to be able to handle increased demands on the business. Based on our advice, they are looking to hire someone to manage operations.

Another potential gap is the lack of relationship-building talent on the team. To grow, the founders need to cultivate relationships with individuals who not only have deep knowledge of the financial-technology sector but who are also influencers in the industry. The team needs someone who can aggressively promote their product outside their existing network.

Blanca is the only one on the team with high Relationship talent. However, she is completely focused on building the product, leaving her with no time to pursue relationships. The investor, who has recently come on board with a million-dollar investment, is well-known in the financial industry — but he is not a promoter.

So the founders have decided to step outside their current networks to recruit their fifth board member — someone with strong Relationship and Selling talents. The idea is for this board member to promote their product but also act as a bridge to other influencers who can help them with critical information and resources.

Using insights from QuantumPro's example, think about how you will build *your* leadership team.

Whether you have a team in place or you are looking for new partners, use the Team Talent Map Tool (See Appendix) to map the talents of your current or potential team members.

Keeping the goals of your venture in mind, make sure to account for all 10 talents of successful builders; they are the demands of the builder role. Most early-stage venture teams are small, with three to five team members, so establish partnerships with people outside your team to make up for the areas where dominant talent is missing from your core team.

Building your team using a talent-based perspective will help you realize the best fit for each team member. But more than just offering role clarity, it will give each member of your team a common language to understand the behaviors of others on the team.

For instance, when Amrita, Jordan and Blanca discussed some of the challenges they will face and decisions they need to make in the near future, they acknowledged that decoding each other's personality made it much easier to make sense of each other's actions and thought processes. Sensitivity to others' emotions fosters understanding, empathy, connection and acceptance among team members. This, in turn, creates a psychologically safe and supportive environment in which the team can afford to take innovative actions and risks without the fear of being judged or punished for failure.

Jordan not having a clear role on the fast-growing team is a sensitive issue for QuantumPro. But an open conversation in a psychologically safe environment about the company's needs and how each member can best contribute made Jordan more receptive to changes in his as well as Amrita's roles. The team is working together to define duties, assign work and establish a chain of command. This is not just Jordan's problem. It is everyone's problem, and the team needs to sort through it in a way that best meets the needs of the growing business. This is a great example of how teams transcend being a group of separate individuals to becoming a whole that is greater than the sum of its parts.

Another benefit of building your team using a talent-based perspective is that it highlights your team's blind spots and pushes you to move beyond familiar and similar connections and search for "outsiders" — diverse members — to join the team. Outsiders are likely to add new knowledge and make connections that you need to grow and scale your business. For instance, QuantumPro is bringing in a new board member who is adept at promoting products and building bridges between networks, thus filling the Relationship talent gap in their team profile.

The best functioning teams combine the personality of their members with the right mix of skills and work experiences. The higher the congruence between skills, experiences and personalities, the stronger the team's performance. What is the point of having the smartest team members if they can't get along?

For instance, you may have a technically and functionally brilliant team member whose personality does not gel with the personalities of others on the team. This will hurt your team's performance. Similarly, you may have harmony among team members, but if you lack diversity in skills and backgrounds, it will negatively affect the team's performance. The team talent map successfully marries the functional requirements of the role (demands that builders have to meet) with insight into the talents needed to fulfill the demands of the role.

Building an Extended Team

Building something from scratch is an uncertain and unpredictable process. One way to tackle unanticipated contingencies when building your venture is by cultivating a wide network of relationships.

Research indicates that successful builders proactively employ strategies that enable them to cross social boundaries and build diverse networks. They co-create with their customers. They build alliances with their investors, suppliers and other strategic partners to reduce uncertainty, acquire resources and bring their ideas to market. And they explore their personal networks (*direct ties*) for *bridging ties* — people who can connect them to out-of-network individuals they want to meet (*indirect ties*).

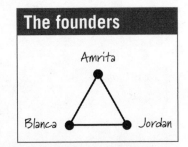

The founders

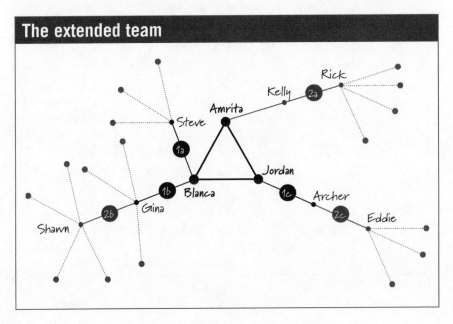

The extended team

QuantumPro's Extended Team

Tie strength (Direct or Indirect)	Connection	Commitment	Timeline	Outcome
Direct tie	1a. Blanca to Steve	Blanca's brother, Steve, is a college recruiter. He will recruit three potential candidates to interview for the role of a software developer.	Next week	Hire first employee (software developer) in four weeks.
Direct tie	1b. Blanca to Gina	Gina, Blanca's college roommate, works at an advertising company. Discuss marketing strategy and budget with her.	Before next Monday	Finalize marketing strategy; allocate funds.
Direct tie	1c. Jordan to Prof. Archer	Jordan's professor, Dr. Archer, is a network theory expert. Discuss Dunbar's number/network theory.	Next 2 weeks	Refine existing algorithm.
Indirect tie	2a. Amrita to Kelly to Rick Leed	Amrita's college roommate, Kelly, is the bridging tie to Rick Leed, a potential investor and financial adviser.	3 months	Seeking a minimum investment of $1 million.
Indirect tie	2b. Blanca to Gina to Shawn	Gina is the bridging tie to Shawn, a potential COO.	Next 4 weeks	Onboard COO by the end of this month.
Indirect tie	2c. Jordan to Archer to Eddie Johnson	Prof. Archer is the bridging tie to a potential board member, Eddie Johnson, an industry expert.	Next 3 months	Fill the fifth seat on the board.

Think of your extended team as a web of affiliations with direct and indirect ties. Your direct ties — people you or your co-founders know personally and frequently interact with — are toward the center of your web of affiliations. Your indirect ties, who you do not know personally but would like to connect with through intermediaries or bridging ties, are farther from the center. The more distant someone is from the center of your web, the more bridging ties it will take to connect with them.

Start by eliciting commitments from your direct ties. Family members, friends, coworkers or members of your personal board of directors may become investors, partners, helpers or employees. These direct ties can give you access to new resources, new ideas or just a helping hand. Pay attention to the gaps in your team talent map, and try to negotiate commitments from your personal network to fill those gaps.

For instance, the QuantumPro founders needed help finding and hiring their first employee, who will make up for the gaps in their team talent profile. Blanca's brother, Steve, is a college recruiter, and he is going to refer a programmer to them. Use the Extended Team Tool (See Appendix) to keep track of the commitments from each member in your personal network.

Identify potential bridging ties in your personal network. Who can connect you to the information and resources you need — human, financial or otherwise — based on their personal or work relationships?

For instance, QuantumPro found its first big investor through Amrita's college roommate who made personal introductions. The roommate was a bridging tie who reduced the distance between the QuantumPro team and a funder in another network who was willing to invest in the financial-technology industry. Likewise, Jordan asked his college professor (a direct tie) to help the team recruit the fifth member to their board, which made the professor another bridging tie. Use the Extended Team Tool (See Appendix) to identify and highlight the bridging ties in your network.

Add members to your team. Employees, suppliers, mentors, advisers, funders or helpers — you will need them all. Keep your team talent profile top of mind as you build your extended team.

For instance, QuantumPro's investor is not only bringing in much-needed financial resources, but he will also help the team manage its budget and focus on profit margin. Only one team member, Jordan, is currently focused on financial matters (Profitability is one of his top four talents). The investor is filling the gaps in Jordan's knowledge about financial matters. He will hold the team financially accountable, which is critical for the survival of an early-stage venture.

The QuantumPro founders also need an industry expert who can speak on their behalf and promote their product. To fill this gap, they are bringing in a new board member. Because the company is growing fast, QuantumPro needs to hire its first employee, a programmer, to help ease Blanca's workload. Looking at their team talent map, it would be wise for QuantumPro to hire a star coder with the following talents:

- **Independence** — a jack-of-all-trades who can pitch in to help when needed

- **Knowledge** — someone who can gather information about the latest technological advances in the financial sector

- **Disruptor** — someone who can be a perfect partner to Blanca in creating new products

Regularly update your team talent map to gauge what you need to grow your venture. Add members who have the talents and skills to fulfill your needs. Diversity of talents and skills is the cornerstone of highly effective teams.

As your team expands, pay attention to the intangibles. Developing an effective team culture is in your hands. Articulate your vision to the team, establish priorities, and communicate clearly and tirelessly. Everyone should know why they are on the team and what they have to do. Share your core values, and live by them.

If your core value is to deliver the highest quality to the customer, then continuously improve your product or service to deliver what you promise. If your core value is to maximize customer engagement, then commit to making engagement part of your business practice. Your team will follow your lead.

Things to Do

1. Build your leadership team with the right mix of skills and talents. Use the team talent map to record each member's talents.

2. Identify your team's greatest strengths and potential gaps. Establish partnerships to make up for blind spots or gaps in your team's talent profile.

3. Identify people in your personal network who can act as bridging ties to new networks and resources.

4. Build diverse networks by reaching across social boundaries. Keep your team talent profile top of mind as you build your extended team.

BUILD YOUR WAY FORWARD

Throughout this book, we have shared stories of builders with you. Some, like Charles Schwab and Stephanie Breedlove, are highly successful, with well-established companies, while others, like Sam, are just beginning their journey.

Sam has decided to expand her service and provide high-quality mobile meals at five different locations on campus to cater to students who don't have time to go to the dining hall. She is also ready to roll out a modified version of Phase 2 from her storyboard.

Her initial idea was to prepare fresh food in front of students with ingredients they pick, thus creating memorable experiences for them. But cooking meals in front of students is time-consuming and labor-intensive. And many students don't have time to wait. So her new idea is to deliver a box of fresh ingredients with a recipe to students so they can "take and bake" the meals in their residence hall kitchen or, for those who live off campus, in their home.

Not only is Sam using what she learned from her experiment to improve her existing products and services and build new ones, but she is also adding new customer segments (students who live off campus) and expanding her customer base.

From exploring opportunities around her to experimenting and modifying her products and services, Sam is well on her way to success. She has taken the first few steps on a 1,000-mile journey.

Like Sam, bring your ideas to life by exploring who you are, what activities and interests resonate with you, and what you can achieve. Learn how to recognize opportunities and build a minimally viable solution to the problem you are trying to solve. Find your first customer, and test and validate your hypotheses.

Make your venture sustainable by building a solid foundation with a leadership team you create by focusing on team members' talents and skills and then expanding your networks. Then you can think about hiring your very first employee, establishing protocols and management practices, and defining your culture.

Make time to dream big, all the while taking small steps toward your long-term goals. Stay in touch with your advisers and mentors; follow the trajectories of successful builders you admire; talk to experts who can counsel you through roadblocks and missteps; and read books, articles and websites that show you how to grow and scale your venture. Continue to improve your product or service, and keep moving toward your next goal. Every step takes you closer to seeing your venture succeed.

Some of you will build a for-profit venture, while others will build a social enterprise. Still others will have a corporate job and look for opportunities to build new products or services. No matter where your journey begins, the principles outlined in this book give you the tools you need to build something that has the potential to be sustainable and lasting.

Building a venture is a journey. Now that you have the tools, you can do this!

What are you building?

Part Three:

THE 10 TALENTS OF
SUCCESSFUL BUILDERS

CONFIDENCE

Key Traits:

- You know yourself and present yourself effectively with confidence.

- You clearly understand and can influence others.

- You are action-oriented and take initiative.

- You have conviction in your ability to be a successful builder.

Highly successful builders have little self-doubt. Rather, they are more likely to possess strong self-belief. If you have high Confidence, you believe that you have what it takes to be a successful builder.

Your certainty in your ability helps you start organizations, persist in the face of ambiguity and failure, and remain confident when meeting challenges as you pursue success. You recognize opportunities and initiate action. While uncertainty may plague others — who endlessly weigh the potential value of an opportunity, gauge the complexities in the environment and fall prey to "analysis paralysis" — you possess a resilient self-belief that leads you to act. And act quickly.

You are so confident in your ability to control the events in your life and to manage your environment effectively that you know you will succeed. Your high Confidence also helps you convince others — investors, customers, prospective employees and potential partners — of your ability to get positive results.

Builders with high Confidence perform well in stressful conditions. You believe that bigger challenges bring greater rewards and that strong, persistent efforts will lead to success. You see little possibility for failure, choose courses of action that you think have a high probability of success and avoid situations where you feel less in control. When others see risk, you see opportunity. When others see roadblocks and potential failure, you see victory.

What's more, as a builder with high Confidence, you like to expand your knowledge base. The more information you have about a particular situation, the less risk you see in pursuing the opportunity. This gives you more confidence in your decisions and improves your likelihood of success.

Your certainty in your ideas and your ability to make things happen motivate you to create and commercialize new products and services. Your strong Confidence talents inspire continuous innovation that helps your organization grow and survive.

Builders with high Confidence assume that growth will continue well into the future. Indeed, you are quite focused on the distant horizon, driven by your unshakeable belief in your ability to build large, successful, mission-driven organizations. You are willing to navigate difficulties as you gradually accumulate human and financial resources, constantly invest in new ideas, expand the organization's knowledge base, and attract better talent to ensure your long-term success. You take your responsibility to steward the organization into the future very seriously.

A word of caution: Builders' confidence and conviction grow organizations, but *overconfidence* can be harmful to an enterprise's health. Sometimes overconfident builders make decisions in haste, underestimating the complexity of the situation. You can avoid jeopardizing your organization's future by slowing down and considering all the relevant factors before making a decision. This is especially true if your organization is in a dynamic industry with a complex environment and a constantly changing landscape.

At times, you can underestimate the resources required for the organization's survival or growth by overestimating your ability to get results with minimal staff, materials and equipment. At other times, you can overcommit resources in pursuit of an idea or opportunity without assessing the competition and market readiness — especially when entering new and untested markets.

What's more, if you are an early mover into a business or nonprofit sector, pay close attention to customer needs and readiness, technological issues, supply chain contingencies, and delivery systems you need to bring the product or service to the market. Paying heed to these issues will prevent you from making mistakes and wasting money and resources — and will increase the likelihood of your organization's survival and growth.

Confidence Talent in Action:

Warren Buffett, CEO and chairman of Berkshire Hathaway: "I always knew I was going to be rich. I don't think I ever doubted it for a minute."

Michael Dell, CEO and chairman of Dell, Inc., when asked, at age 19, what he wanted to do with his life, told his dad: "Compete with IBM."

Malcolm Gladwell, author of *The Tipping Point* and *Blink*, explaining overconfidence: "As novices, we don't trust our judgment. Then we have some success, and begin to feel a little surer of ourselves. Finally, we get to the top of our game and succumb to the trap of thinking that there's nothing we can't master. As we get older and more experienced, we overestimate the accuracy of our judgments, especially when the task before us is difficult and when we're involved with something of great personal importance."

Maximizing Your Confidence Talent:

1. *Plan ahead to boost your confidence.* Create an elaborate business or nonprofit plan with rich details. Project multiple scenarios, run analysis and outline resource needs before taking action. Set milestones and outcome expectations for each stage of a project. Prepare for contingencies. While you are already confident in your ability to be successful, thorough planning can validate and support your certainty and help you achieve your objectives.

2. *Do your homework.* To make your product or service ready for the market, collect as much information as you can about industry or nonprofit sector specifications, procedures and documents, competitors, value proposition to customers, intellectual property protection issues, and technological requirements.

3. *Avoid the "speed trap."* Don't let your strong sense of self-belief and initiative push you to make decisions under pressure. When the window of opportunity is narrow and you have to make decisions quickly, pause to reinforce your certainty by considering your experiences, knowledge and what-if scenarios before you take action.

4. *Discuss opportunities with your network.* Consider your self-image in these discussions. You are sure of yourself and easily influence others. But your network ties can help you assess opportunities in a different light. Listen to their points of view to get a more complete picture of the situation. People you know can also help you access resources to pursue those opportunities.

5. *Avoid "in-group" thinking.* Your self-confidence and strong desire for control may cause you to surround yourself with people who are not likely to challenge your thinking. Seek feedback from diverse stakeholders — managers, senior executives, board members and investors. Their alternative outlooks on risks and opportunities will stimulate your sound decision-making.

DELEGATOR

Key Traits:

- You readily delegate authority and responsibility.

- You proactively collaborate with others.

- You recognize and draw on people's special abilities.

- You help ensure that team members become effective contributors.

Highly successful builders quickly adjust to accommodate the changing needs and new realities of a growing organization. If you are a Delegator, you understand that a rapidly growing venture needs capabilities and resources beyond what you alone can provide.

Delegators work *on* the organization rather than *in* it. You recognize that a growing organization requires a shift from a do-it-yourself style, which is helpful in the early stages, to a more hands-off approach as the business or nonprofit starts to grow. You are well aware that you cannot possibly accomplish everything yourself, and you are willing to relinquish control and hand off authority for certain tasks to others who are better equipped to handle them.

You have mastered the art of delegation. This frees up your time to focus on activities that yield the highest returns for the organization and cause it to grow.

You develop team capacity and delegate wisely. You understand your employees' capabilities and strengths and position them to take responsibility for tasks at which they are most likely to excel. You also give employees autonomy to make decisions related to their tasks, which fosters psychological ownership and engagement. Engaged and motivated employees are more likely to take initiative to build better systems and streamline work processes, thus increasing productivity and benefitting the organization.

Simply put, effective Delegators are great managers and supportive bosses. You set clear expectations about timing, budget and deliverables; make sure employees have the tools and resources they need to do their jobs; provide opportunities for training and learning; and genuinely care about the growth of each individual. You seek input from your employees and value their opinions and expertise.

What's more, you encourage new ideas and approaches to getting things done, and you focus on outcomes rather than processes. You recognize employees for a job well done, thus creating an atmosphere of mutual respect and trust. Effective delegation increases employee commitment, boosts morale and positively influences organizational performance.

A word of caution: While you delegate effectively, *do not abdicate* your overall responsibility for a project. The buck stops with you. Remember to set milestones to monitor progress, and communicate frequently with the people to whom you are delegating to avoid costly mistakes or surprises. When they complete tasks, provide feedback about what worked and what didn't. Set up a successful delegation process. In the long run, this will build employee capacity and, more importantly, save you time — time you can use to create new opportunities for your organization.

Delegator Talent in Action:

Carol Loomis, former editor-at-large at *Fortune*, on Warren Buffett: "As long as numbers are looking as they should, though, Buffett does not poke into operations, but rather leaves his managers free to run their businesses as their intelligence tells them to."

Charlie Munger, vice chairman of Berkshire Hathaway: "We chose our style of operation to fit our natures, which demanded that plenty of time be spent thinking and learning. Naturally, this caused extreme delegation. Warren [Buffett] and I avoid doing anything that someone else at Berkshire can do better."

Scott Heiferman, co-founder and CEO of Meetup.com: "Avoid thinking that you have to do it all. Divide and conquer. Do what you are best at and let others take care of the rest. Each founder should focus on his or her strengths."

Maximizing Your Delegator Talent:

1. *Identify what to delegate.* Make a detailed list of all the activities on your plate. Ask yourself two questions as you go through the list: 1. Is this activity critical for the growth of my organization? 2. Is there someone else who can do it better? Strategic planning, managing important customer relationships, hiring decisions and confidential tasks are critical duties that usually require your direct attention. On the other hand, for accounting, legal work, social media, IT functions and administrative tasks, there is usually someone else who can do it better, so delegate those tasks.

2. *Identify whom to delegate to.* If you have hired people with the right talents and skills, then it will be easy for you to identify the right person for each task. Match the job to the individual with the appropriate expertise to deliver results, not just to those who aren't busy.

3. *Take time to set things up for success.* One of the main hurdles to delegation is the amount of time it takes to train someone. It is worth your time to make sure employees have what they need to do the job right. Give others clear instructions and enough time to complete tasks.

4. *Allow employees to perform, and give them feedback.* Be patient. Effective delegation builds the capacity of your team. Manage the process by focusing on the results. Set clear milestones for key stages of each project, and monitor employees' progress. Talk to them about what works and what does not. As they learn to fine-tune their actions, they will improve their performance on each task and be able to take on more responsibility.

5. *Use your network to access the human resources you need for delegation.* If hiring new employees is not an option, borrow or barter resources to keep costs in check.

DETERMINATION

Key Traits:

- You push to achieve and have a tremendous work ethic.

- You confront obstacles directly and overcome them.

- You are persistent and undeterred by failures or roadblocks.

- You are eager to make decisions and quick to act.

Highly successful builders have a high *adversity quotient* — the ability to recover from setbacks. If you have high Determination, you believe that you can confront and overcome insurmountable obstacles.

Builders with high Determination don't give up when the going gets tough. Delays and obstructions don't discourage you. Your tenacity and persistence allow you to recover from setbacks and failures. Whether confronted by a failed project, an unsuccessful product launch or a disastrous end to a new venture, you know how to pick yourself up and resume your efforts. You strongly believe that you can overcome any obstacle by working harder.

You believe that you have the capacity to control your circumstances, and you are highly motivated to change adversity into opportunity by taking action. Instead of giving in to feelings of frustration and anger when you encounter obstacles, you see beyond the roadblocks and visualize a better future. Your optimistic attitude helps you achieve desired organizational outcomes.

You take personal accountability for the consequences of your choices and actions, and doing so mobilizes you to act. You strongly believe that your setbacks and failures are the result of a lack of effort on your part, and you are willing to do whatever it takes to fix things. This compels you to double your efforts, try new options and push forward when faced with adversity.

Builders with high Determination tenaciously pursue goals. You identify opportunities, take initiative and persevere when faced with obstacles. You are focused on winning and will not take no for an answer. This attitude helps you launch new organizations, enter new markets or nonprofit sectors, and invent new products or services despite formidable barriers.

Further, you have a high tolerance for stress and an immense capacity for sustained hard work. You confront every situation with robust energy and stamina; setbacks and obstacles strengthen your resolve to remain on task and work harder. Your ability to put in long hours ensures that your organization survives through numerous ups and downs.

A word of caution: Builders with high tenacity and perseverance can have a misplaced commitment to a selected course of action. In other words, you may have a tendency to stick with a failing strategy or continue allocating resources to a pet project or product, even when the results are consistently below expectations. You are also likely to harbor deep discontent, disappointment and regret when faced with a failing venture or an unsuccessful launch. Because of your extremely high expectations for success, extraordinary dedication and complete investment in your organization, any outcome that doesn't meet your expectations can trigger regretful thinking.

In addition, you routinely make tough calls in the course of running your organization — for instance, firing employees, litigating with competitors to protect intellectual property, negotiating late payments with financiers or sorting disputes with suppliers. Having to make unpleasant decisions comes at a great personal cost to the highly vested builder. Understand that despite your extreme commitment to your venture, you might not attain all of your organizational goals. Keep close tabs on outcomes, and adjust your strategy if necessary.

Determination Talent in Action:

Thomas Edison, American inventor and businessman: "I have not failed. I've just found 10,000 ways that won't work."

Richard Branson, founder of Virgin: "If you are hurt, lick your wounds and get up again. If you've given it your absolute best, it's time to move forward."

Wang Chuanfu, founder and CEO of BYD, the Chinese electric battery and electric car maker, when asked by Warren Buffett how BYD would sustain its lead in the market: "We'll never, never rest."

Maximizing Your Determination Talent:

1. *Share your optimistic outlook with your partners, employees and investors.* You see possibilities where others see barriers. Your determined optimism and work ethic will inspire and energize your team to do more.

2. *Partner with creative individuals.* Working with inventive people can inspire and energize you. Your uncanny ability to sort through many ideas and hone in on the best one will help transform their idea into a product or service for a customer.

3. *Always keep the big picture in mind, and monitor your progress toward predefined goals.* This will help you navigate through the twists and turns of the builder journey and strengthen your natural tendency to push forward in adverse circumstances. When executing a strategy, set specific milestones so you know if the strategy is working or if you need to change course. This way, you can avoid costly mistakes early.

4. *Be attentive to the constantly shifting business or nonprofit landscape.* Your tenacity to see a pet project or product through may blind you to changes in the market. Pay close attention to new technologies, a changing customer base, and emerging new business or nonprofit models. Staying aware of your market or sector environment will help you switch gears if necessary.

5. *Don't focus on the cause of setbacks.* Rather, direct your energy toward activities that can help you move forward. Setbacks and challenges are part of the builder journey. Improving your reaction to adverse circumstances will keep you upbeat and reduce downtime when you do encounter obstacles.

6. *Keep things in perspective.* Making tough calls is part of running an organization. Don't dwell on unpleasant decisions. Rely on your support system — business or organizational partners, investors, mentors and family members — to help you deal with the personal toll these decisions can take on you.

7. *Reflect on your successes and failures.* Set aside time to analyze why a decision yielded positive or negative results. Replicate the positive, and weed out the actions or behaviors that produced negative outcomes. Over time, you will build a repertoire of skills to make effective business decisions.

DISRUPTOR

Key Traits:

- You imagine beyond the boundaries of what exists now.

- You explore options and can think your way through problems.

- You constantly dream up new products or services for customers.

- You have a mind that is typically firing with many different ideas.

- You are a curious and quick learner.

Highly successful builders can creatively look beyond the present and imagine possible futures for their organization. If you are a Disruptor, you are driven to steer your organization in new directions.

Whether introducing new products and services, entering untapped markets or nonprofit sectors, or initiating innovative technologies or production processes, you are constantly thinking of new ways to propel your organization forward. Comfortable with the unknown and the unfamiliar, you always look for new ways to combine and recombine resources to create innovative solutions for your customers. Your creative action renews your organization's value proposition and differentiates your organization from your competitors. It also enables you to disrupt markets by introducing new and unexpected products and services or by developing novel methods of doing business.

Disruptors are alert to changes in the external business or nonprofit environment — new technologies, shifts in customer or societal needs, industry trends, or competitor actions. You constantly evaluate new possibilities, revise your expectations of the imagined future and formulate fresh action plans to achieve your goals. This endless cycle of new information, new opportunities and new action plans helps you start ventures or grow existing ones.

As a Disruptor, you are quick to act. You seize opportunities and are usually the first mover in the market. Your unique ability to take an idea and quickly transform it into a product or service that generates revenue or has an inspiring mission helps you stay ahead of the competition. And your proactivity garners your organization high profits, allowing you to establish your brand and capture market share ahead of others in the industry.

Highly disruptive builders are rule breakers who don't like to conform to the norms and traditions of their industries or sectors. You refuse to be bogged down by established practices, bureaucratic structures or arcane business processes. You like to work autonomously, outside established organizational practices, where you can think and create freely.

You constantly push the boundaries, always experimenting with new ideas to sort the good from the bad. It is this ability to experiment, usually in the face of acute uncertainty, that gives you the potential to generate innovative paths to success.

A word of caution: While disruptive builders are independent spirits who like to work autonomously, implementing ideas requires working with a team. Lack of communication with your team or too much separation from ongoing operations can hurt the development and integration of new products or services into an existing organization. Make sure to communicate your ideas and strategies to your team. Sharing will increase the likelihood of launching a successful product or service.

In addition, you may fall prey to "incumbent inertia" as you achieve success and grow. Don't become complacent with growth. Maintain the organizational flexibility that allowed you to explore your creative imagination in the first place. Continue to pay attention to changing customer needs, evolving technologies, and the shifting business or nonprofit environment. Remember, this endless stream of new information and knowledge will fuel your creativity.

Be careful not to rush to launch new initiatives. Your creative tendency might cause you to experiment and launch multiple initiatives at the same time. This perceived lack of focus may hamper your chances of success. Don't lose sight of your core business or your organization's main mission and purpose.

Disruptor Talent in Action:

Jeff Bezos, founder and CEO of Amazon.com: "If you double the number of experiments you do per year, you're going to double your inventiveness. The thing about inventing is you have to be both stubborn and flexible, more or less simultaneously. If you're not stubborn, you'll give up on experiments too soon. And if you're not flexible, you'll pound your head against the wall and you won't see a different solution to a problem you're trying to solve."

Marissa Mayer, former president and CEO of Yahoo and former vice president of search products at Google: "The 'Googly' thing is to launch it [a product] early on Google Labs and then iterate, learning what the market wants — and making it great. The beauty of experimenting in this way is that you never get too far from what the market wants. The market pulls you back."

James Dyson, design engineer and founder of Dyson: "We are all looking for the magic formula. Well, here you go: Creativity + Iterative Development = Innovation."

Maximizing Your Disruptor Talent:

1. *Balance current and future customer needs.* It is easy to be tied down with day-to-day organizational management and focused on delivering what your customers expect from you. Set aside time to disconnect from the present, and feed your creativity to imagine your customers' future needs. This will help you dream and plan for the future and maintain your competitive advantage.

2. *Use measurement to evaluate your ideas.* When weighing which idea to implement, ask yourself, "How can we measure this?" Pick ideas apart to identify issues that could crop up during implementation. If the results show that a project isn't viable, then modify or abandon the idea and move on to the next one.

3. *Minimize potential pitfalls by releasing your new product or service incrementally.* Implementing new ideas is risky. Iteration is key. Launch the prototype, gather feedback from customers, make necessary changes and test again. Using this low-cost approach, you can turn your novel and creative ideas into products or services without much potential downside.

4. *Maintain a simple organizational structure.* Fewer layers of hierarchy will enable smoother information flow between you and your team. A simple organizational structure will also increase employee involvement in implementing ideas, encourage employees' creativity, and lead to quicker execution and understanding of new ideas.

5. *Balance efficiency with creativity.* Process management techniques, such as total quality management or Six Sigma, which can increase your growing organization's efficiency and productivity, are also likely to decrease your ability to innovate. Don't let efficiency-enhancing practices act as barriers to exploring new ideas. Nurture your natural Disruptor talent. Continue to invest in new ideas as you increase operational efficiency.

6. *Mobilize resources to fuel your innovation process.* You need two things for successful innovation and market disruption: diverse experiences that spark your creativity and resources to drive the innovation process. Tap in to your existing network or build new alliances internally and externally to stimulate your creativity and access shared resources.

7. *Learn from your failures.* When carefully planned new initiatives fail, the potential to learn from them is immense. Don't let this learning opportunity go to waste. Conduct a post-mortem, make sense of what happened and add what you have learned to your knowledge base. Fostering *intelligent failures* will help you learn what not to do as you dream about the future.

INDEPENDENCE

Key Traits:

- You depend on yourself to get the job done.

- You have a strong sense of responsibility.

- You can handle multiple tasks successfully.

- You are resolute, with a high level of competence in every aspect of managing an organization.

Highly successful builders strongly believe they can take an idea from concept to creation based on their efforts alone. If you have high Independence talent, you consider yourself a jack-of-all-trades who can single-handedly start and operate an organization.

Builders with Independence talent like to launch ventures. Your ability to multitask and your extremely strong sense of responsibility help you tackle the basics of starting an organization on your own. From recognizing opportunities and gathering resources to building networks and implementing strategies, you can do it all. Your self-reliance greatly increases an early-stage organization's odds of survival.

As a builder with high Independence, you autonomously set goals and take action to achieve them. You have high expectations of success that push you to develop specific strategies to attain your desired outcomes. You firmly believe that your actions decide the fate of your organization. Consequently, you are motivated to make things happen. Your can-do attitude explains your early builder success.

You actively access tangible resources — real estate, workspace, communication infrastructure or marketing materials — as well as intangible ones — brand name, technological capability, organizational processes, customer relationships or organizational culture — to start and grow a new venture. And to ensure that the venture operates efficiently and effectively, you proficiently maximize all these resources.

You are extremely committed to your organization. Starting an enterprise is a grueling process, and your reserves of high energy and a vast capacity for hard work enable you to make it happen. Your wholehearted dedication to your new organization ensures its survival and success.

Dealing with the unknown and uncertain energizes you. Early-stage organizations are rife with ambiguity and day-to-day challenges. Your ability to think and act quickly allows you to develop creative solutions to complex problems. Your agile mind can quickly make modifications to your business or nonprofit plan, product or service mix, customer base, resource needs, and implementation strategies as needed.

A word of caution: Independence is critical in the startup phase as you translate an idea into an operational organization with minimal help. But, as the venture begins to flourish, the desire for complete autonomy and control over every aspect of the organization can hinder its growth. Go-it-alone builders can get things done, but that trait can keep you from focusing on activities that bring the highest value to a growing organization. In addition, 20-hour days packed with multiple tasks could lead to burnout, jeopardizing the very survival of the venture.

As your organization grows, it is impossible to do everything yourself. Develop processes and systems to handle repetitive tasks. Hire and train your staff, and then transfer certain responsibilities to them. Keep checks in place to ensure things are on track. Having the right people and processes in place will keep you in control of your organization without personally handling every task.

Independence Talent in Action:

Mona Simpson about her brother, Steve Jobs (1955-2011), co-founder, chairman and CEO of Apple: "He was never embarrassed about working hard, even if the results were failures."

Sachin Kamdar, co-founder and CEO of Parse.ly: "The role of a CEO almost changes every single month as your company grows … one day you could find yourself being an account manager, the next day you're a salesperson, the next day you're HR and recruiting, the next day you're a marketer. It's honestly been a challenge to deal with all these different things you have to as CEO of the company and trying to manage yourself and your time."

Chad Hurley, co-founder and former CEO of YouTube: "As you start building the product, don't assume that you know all the answers. Be prepared to adapt. You may have initial thoughts or ideas on how something will work but you need to observe how you and the community are using it. Don't be afraid to change direction midcourse."

Maximizing Your Independence Talent:

1. *Plan for the long term, and don't lose sight of your main objective.* Your complete focus on the here and now will ensure the survival of your venture. It is easy to get lost in the day-to-day minutiae. But make sure your short-term goals align with your long-term objectives for the ultimate success and longevity of your organization. Set clear criteria to make sure you are on the right track in the early stages. Stay focused on the reason you started the venture in the first place.

2. *Be prepared to pivot quickly.* Pay attention to your competition, customer segment, technology, business regulations, and the business or nonprofit environment. The more you know, the quicker you'll be able to adapt to changing circumstances.

3. *Form strategic alliances and a diverse network.* While you have a natural tendency to be autonomous, connections can help you secure resources in the early stages of your organization — resources you may not have direct ownership of or access to. In addition, a diverse network increases your likelihood of reaching a broader audience for your new products, services or mission.

4. *Don't develop builder myopia.* Resist falling in love with your idea or product. Try to be objective about the product or service you want to offer to the market. Assess the market need, be aware of the competition and understand your target customer. Develop a product, service or mission that aligns with your customers' needs.

5. *Hire staff members who can meet the needs of your growing organization.* As your organization expands and your offerings in the market diversify, realize that you will have to delegate. Be sure to hire employees who have talents and skills that fit your organization. This will free you up to work on things that grow your organization.

KNOWLEDGE

Key Traits:

- You push yourself to acquire in-depth information about every aspect of your organization.

- You use knowledge as a competitive advantage.

- You have a preoccupation with your organization that borders on obsession.

- You anticipate knowledge needs and use knowledge well.

Highly successful builders are obsessed with their organization; they have a strong desire to acquire in-depth knowledge about all aspects of it. If you have high Knowledge talent, you constantly search for new information and experiences to navigate your organization in a highly complex business or nonprofit environment.

Starting and growing an organization is a formidable task. The demands on the builder are many: mapping the industry landscape, understanding what products and services to offer, raising capital, managing employees and customers, and competing in a global economy. You inherently understand that *knowledge* is a valuable asset. You use your vast knowledge to analyze complex business or nonprofit environments, solve problems, select the best course of action, and stay ahead of the competition.

As a builder with high Knowledge talent, you plumb your deep reservoirs of learning to enter new markets and to compete more effectively in the existing market. You gather an incredible amount of information and store every new fact, fresh piece of data and new experience in your mental library, constantly asking yourself, "What does this mean for my organization?" This accumulation of knowledge greatly increases your chances of finding and exploiting discoveries that others may miss.

What's more, you can foresee the utility of products, services, or mission and purpose that the market is not yet expecting. Just as Henry Ford upended the transportation market by introducing the mass-produced automobile and Steve Jobs' iPad disrupted the traditional PC market, you systematically apply knowledge to innovate disruptively.

You also use your encyclopedic Knowledge talent to keep competition at bay, which helps you gain precious market share and maintain continued profitability. For instance, you might learn about intellectual property law to guard against competitors imitating your discoveries. Similarly, you strive to obtain information about new production processes, technologies, bundling of services, or business or nonprofit models to give you a competitive advantage.

Builders with high Knowledge talent assess and manage risk effectively. Builders have to make decisions in highly complex environments with incomplete information, which entails much risk. Your ability to collect and process a lot of information gives you a better understanding of your environment. Whether you have to make a decision about releasing a new product or service, rolling out a new marketing strategy, introducing a new production process, or meeting a burning societal need, you understand the implications of the choices you face. And you calculate the inherent risk of each option and select the best course of action.

You have superior insight into your customers' needs. Constantly driven to gather knowledge about the business or nonprofit environment, you quickly recognize trends in consumer behavior and effectively reallocate organizational resources to cater to changing customer expectations. This behavior turns your customers into advocates and generates higher revenue for your business or passion for your nonprofit organization.

In short, builders with high Knowledge talent never stop learning. Your ability to absorb knowledge and information gives your organization a much higher chance of survival and growth.

A word of caution: As a builder with high Knowledge talent, you possess intellectual curiosity that may generate *too many* new ideas and insights. You might pivot from one idea to the next — sometimes too quickly — confusing your employees and customers. This can hamper day-to-day decision-making as teams grapple with constant change in direction and incoherent strategy.

Knowing how to differentiate between ideas that truly improve your organization and those that do not is the key. Select the ideas that streamline your organization and add value for your customers. Avoid the lure of implementing every idea and insight without measured reflection.

Knowledge Talent in Action:

Paul B. Allen, founder of Ancestry.com: "I devoured every article and news release and case study I could find on dot-com companies. I believe I read cover to cover nearly every issue of *The Industry Standard, Red Herring, Business 2.0, Wired, Upside* and several other internet publications. I scoured dozens of reports from Jupiter Communications and from leading stock market analysts. I attended dozens of industry conferences and events. And I filtered all the information and ideas I learned about through a simple lens: 'How would this work in genealogy and with families?' It was our ability and insatiable desire to learn and experiment in a fast-moving environment that made us the world leader in online genealogy."

Michael Goldberg, president of Berkshire Hathaway Credit Corp., on Warren Buffett: "He is constantly examining all that he hears: 'Is it consistent and plausible? Is it wrong?' He has a model in his head of the whole world. The computer there compares every new fact with all that he's ever experienced and knows about — and says, 'What does this mean for us?' For Berkshire, that is."

Thane Stenner, founder of Stenner Investment Partners, on successful builders: "There always seems to be a common thread amongst this uncommonly well-to-do subset. They all have a different story, a different path. However, what is a common trait in virtually all of them is that they are 'intellectually curious.' They love to learn. They look for insights, always a better way of doing things … an 'edge.'"

Maximizing Your Knowledge Talent:

1. *Feed your voracious desire to know everything related to your organization.* Read new material on industry-specific websites; in trade publications, annual reports and newsletters; and on social media. Write and share ideas and insights with others, and brainstorm with those inside and outside your organization. Learning everything you can will help you cultivate expertise in different aspects of your organization.

2. *Set aside plenty of time for thinking and learning.* Delegate tasks to others. Free up your time from the daily minutiae to focus on things that help grow your organization.

3. *Sort through your insights before taking action.* Your vast knowledge base generates many ideas. Focus on the truly important and meaningful ones that will move your organization forward.

4. *Get an outsider's point of view.* Your immense depth of knowledge makes you confident in the viability of your ideas. Consider sharing your insights with someone who can challenge your assumptions and provide feedback on the feasibility of your ideas.

5. *Give your employees clear direction.* Your considerable intellectual ability might lead you to change the direction of your organization rapidly. Constant change can confuse your employees. Create a road map they can follow.

PROFITABILITY

Key Traits:

- You are profit-oriented.

- You establish clear goals and objectively measure progress toward those goals.

- You judge the value of an opportunity, a relationship or a decision by its effect on your organization.

- You invest time in planning growth strategies.

- You align employee responsibilities with your organization's goals.

Highly successful builders are fascinated by numbers and money. If you have high Profitability talent, making money is your primary objective.

As a builder with high Profitability talent, you have sharp business instincts, and you use them to price products or services to guarantee a profit on each sale. Consistent with your emphasis on money, you run a tight ship, keeping a close check on operational costs. You make all decisions, big and small, with cost in mind and evaluate your decisions through the prism of profitability. You constantly ask yourself, "How will this affect my bottom line?" Your focus on running the organization efficiently makes you impatient with unnecessary costs caused by delays, detours or obstacles.

Your attitude toward data reflects your penchant for numbers. Your high Profitability talent gives you an uncanny ability to look at the same data that your managers, co-founders or employees have reviewed and come up with unique insights that they may have missed. Numbers are your lifeline. From weekly target meetings to monthly tracks to quarterly company reviews, numbers are the topic of discussion. Not only do you relentlessly measure all aspects of the organization, you know how each number is derived and what day-to-day team member actions affect these numbers.

You also have a long-term view of the enterprise. With a futuristic outlook, you energize yourself and your team members by painting your vision of what the organization will be like months and years from now — and you do it often. Even though monthly and quarterly scrutiny is important, you are focused on the long-term drivers of success and invest a lot of time planning for this future state.

You set targets — financial and non-financial — for the month, quarter, year and decade. Once you have set the targets, you innately understand what steps to take and what levers to pull to achieve them. Then you continuously monitor and measure the results, benchmarking them against the best in the industry. This gives you an objective view of how well the organization is doing.

You don't stop with just setting and monitoring goals. You move on to the most critical step: getting your team on board and helping each team member understand how their daily actions drive the numbers. As a builder with high Profitability talent, you instinctively know how to align employee responsibilities with company goals by finding the right job fit for each employee. And you align each employee's responsibilities with their innate talents so each individual can bring their best self to the job every day.

A word of caution: In your drive to maximize profits, you can sometimes lose sight of your customers. Remember to make customer orientation part of your business philosophy. Encourage your team to focus on increasing customer satisfaction along with the push to maximize revenues.

In addition, be cognizant of your team members' morale. A relentless focus on profitability and a competitive cost culture put immense pressure on employees to maintain the highest levels of performance. Communicate your vision of the future clearly and often to keep the troops energized and morale high.

Along the same lines, never let your employees forget that you value their hard work. Recognizing them for their contributions, big and small, builds loyalty and commitment to the organization and pushes them to perform at higher levels. Engaged employees' energy and effort will pull the organization through tough times.

Profitability Talent in Action:

Warren Buffett, CEO and chairman of Berkshire Hathaway: "Whenever I read about some company undertaking a cost-cutting program, I know it's not a company that really knows what costs are all about. Spurts don't work in this area. The really good manager does not wake up in the morning and say, 'This is the day I'm going to cut costs' any more than he wakes up and decides to practice breathing."

Larry Page, co-founder and CEO of Google: "Our goal is long-term growth in revenue and absolute profit — so we invest aggressively in future innovation while tightly managing our short-term costs."

Bill Gates, co-founder of Microsoft, business magnate, philanthropist and inventor: "Warren [Buffett] and I have the most fun when we're taking the same data that everybody else has and coming up with new ways of looking at them that are both novel and, in a sense, obvious. Each of us tries to do this all the time for our respective companies, but it's particularly enjoyable and stimulating to discuss these insights with each other."

Maximizing Your Profitability Talent:

1. *Use specific timelines and yardsticks to measure your organizational goals.* Applying precise measures will help you track the numbers and gauge how well your organization is moving toward your goals.

2. *Manage your time carefully.* As a builder, you have many demands on your time. Make a list of well-defined initiatives that require your full attention. Reject proposals that don't further your organizational and financial goals.

3. *Write down your vision for the short term and long term, and refer to it often.* Putting your vision in writing and revisiting it regularly will keep you feeling in control and on track.

4. *Communicate your short-term and long-term goals consistently to your employees and clients.* Create a vivid road map for them to follow. Outline your strategies, and include examples, stories, action plans and mock-ups. Help others see the future along with you. Your employees and customers must be able to see the organization through your eyes. It will help them stay emotionally engaged. Work with them to define that future.

5. *Don't lose sight of the human element in business.* Your decisions and your extreme focus on profitability affect your employees and customers. Remember that you are working with people and not just spreadsheets and data.

6. *To help you set realistic organizational goals, learn everything you can about all aspects of your organization.* Read trade journals, industry-specific publications and technological breakthroughs related to your organization. Talk to experts in your area.

RELATIONSHIP

Key Traits:

- You have high social awareness.

- You attract and maintain a constituency.

- You build mutually beneficial relationships.

- You use your relationship talents to access internal and external resources.

- You forge relationships with employees and customers that go beyond work.

- You have an open demeanor, a positive attitude and personal integrity that help build trust.

Highly successful builders have strong interpersonal skills that allow them to build a robust and diversified personal network. If you have high Relationship talent, you inherently understand that running a successful organization is a collective effort that requires interacting with a range of people: suppliers and potential investors, employees and customers, peers, competitors, public officials, and members of the media.

Builders with high Relationship talent take a twofold approach: You use your social ties to access critical resources (financial and non-financial) for your organization. And you use your networks to gain information, share experiences, exchange ideas, pool expertise, draw mutual support and help sustain motivation, thus increasing the likelihood of your organization's survival and success.

You instinctively know how to respond to and engage with those who are critical to your success — customers, employees and suppliers. Using personalized interactions, an ability to accurately perceive customer needs and an accessible attitude, you generate trust and confidence in your brand. You make sure that you retain your best customers, and thus the market share, by creating an emotional bond with them.

Similarly, builders with high Relationship talent create workplaces that have a shared sense of purpose and that connect employees on an emotional level. Your optimism and high personal integrity help build trust and loyalty with employees, motivating them to give more of themselves to their role.

Your social competence also helps you form mutually trusting relationships with your suppliers. These connections encourage both parties to go beyond contractual obligations and result in long-term relationships. You consider your suppliers to be partners, and you invest equity *and* trust in them. You maintain these lasting relationships with your partners by giving them clear requirements for products or services you need, aggressive cost-reduction targets, and competitive pricing — and by demonstrating a willingness to share risk in case of unforeseen events.

Your authenticity and confidence in what you know help you secure financial resources for your organization. You can clearly articulate the future state of your organization and the resources you need to bring your ideas to fruition. Investors respond to your confidence and integrity. People in your network are willing to do more for you than is expected of them.

Your keen social competence also allows you to extract information from your networks. You know what you can get, from whom and when. You share experiences, exchange ideas and make new contacts with people inside and outside your industry. These interactions help you discover new technologies, markets and processes and may result in new partnership opportunities — all essential for the growth of your organization.

The breadth and depth of your networks empower you to confidently and aggressively take risks, try something new, and bear losses and failures. Failure can be extremely painful for you, both financially and psychologically. But your strong and diversified network is a source of emotional support and builds your confidence in times of loss or failure. Your network is a social safety net that can soften the pain and cost of failure, help diminish feelings of isolation, and provide inspiration for fresh business and organizational ideas.

A word of caution: The very ties that help grow organizations can sometimes hamper growth. Three things to be wary about:

- Bigger is not always better. Highly successful builders don't necessarily have larger networks. Be selective about the associations you form. Your confidence in knowing what to expect from whom and how to get it helps you garner resources for your venture.

- Overinvestment in your network may take precious time away from focusing on your organization. Invest your time wisely.

- Sometimes strong networks can shut out new people and new thinking, insulating you from fresh input from the "outside." Just as real capital becomes less productive with age, your social capital can become old and stagnant. It needs regular maintenance and investment. Changing organizational needs will require you to retain the ties that work, abolish those that become obsolete or non-productive, and forge new ones. Remember, introducing new elements into your network will generate new experiences and positive change.

Relationship Talent in Action:

Roy Spence, chairman, CEO and co-founder of marketing communications and advertising company GSD&M: "The key to long-term meaningful, and yes happy and fun, success is to create partnerships of purpose with people you like and who like you. I never did understand the idea of 'don't do business with your friends.' I love building relationships with people who love building something special and making money by making a difference."

David Bradford, lawyer turned tech guru and serial builder: "I can't think of anything more fun than connecting people. People make businesses happen. It's that simple."

Maximizing Your Relationship Talent:

1. *Diversify your networks.* Go beyond your *vertical* ties (people in your immediate circle and those you know well) to cultivate *horizontal* (your competitors, customers and suppliers) and *lateral* ties (builders from unrelated organizations and people outside the business or nonprofit world such as media personnel and government officials).

2. *Remember that reciprocity is vital to maintaining strong relationships.* Offer help, connect people with each other, or share industry or nonprofit-sector information. Others will respond when you need help.

3. *Be selective in whom you invest the most time.* Spend time with your most important customers, your most productive employees and those who can make the most difference to your organization. These relationships will render returns in the immediate future and in the long term.

4. *Understand the local social landscape.* Pay attention to the existing bonds, loyalties and networks that characterize the community where you work and live. Recognize the norms, values and preferences that shape the behavior of the people in your community. This will help you form a durable and effective network that you can maximize for your organization's interests.

5. *Use your time, brand and resources to address social issues.* Build a constituency — a collection of people who have shared beliefs, interests and ambitions. Remember that your customers and employees are part of your community. Collaborating with them on solving social problems will turn them into engaged advocates of your organization and make them your most powerful allies.

6. *Renew and reshape your networks frequently.* Place people who are critical to your organization and who you keep in touch with in your *active network*. Nurture these relationships carefully. Put contacts whose usefulness has diminished over time into your *inactive network*. Prune this list aggressively and often. Your *potential network* is a list of new connections that are vital to the future of your organization. Figure out strategies to build these connections.

RISK

Key Traits:

- You have a strong personality, charisma and confidence.
- You are enthusiastic when taking on challenges.
- You have a highly optimistic perception of risk.
- You make decisions easily in complex situations.
- You take a rational approach to decision-making.

Contrary to popular belief, highly successful builders are not risk seekers; they are risk *mitigators* par excellence. If you have dominant Risk talent, you instinctively know how to manage high-risk situations.

When encountering a challenging decision, you take an analytical approach, meticulously gathering as much information as you can, weighing all the options and assessing everything that can possibly go wrong. Replacing emotion with a rational thought process helps you overcome fear; calculate your odds of success; and decide whether to assume risks such as committing resources to new projects, introducing new products and services, entering new markets, or investing in new technologies.

You tackle uncertainty and risk by working hard to collect every bit of information possible. From tracking past performance to number crunching and creating what-if scenarios, you determine the least risky solution to your organizational challenges. Your investment in acquiring information helps you make smarter choices so you can be ultra-confident about the outcome.

Once you are certain of your choice, you are willing to put everything on the line for it. To an outside observer, this behavior may seem risky, but to you, the decision is well-thought-through and thus carries no risk.

Builders with high Risk talent are avid problem solvers. Your love for what you do and an intense desire to succeed keep you motivated to spend long hours working on a challenging problem. You solve problems analytically. Consequently, you can see patterns and make connections between seemingly unconnected phenomena. This gives you the ability to recognize opportunities and take advantage of market gaps before your competitors do.

You have a belief, sometimes exaggerated, in your ability to control the destiny and future of your venture. This internal locus of control motivates you to take action when things are not going well. You are quick to pursue alternative options when you encounter setbacks. Your will to win remains undiminished even after a painful defeat.

A word of caution: Some extremely successful builders with dominant Risk talent hold themselves in high regard. This phenomenon is known as *hyper-core self-evaluation* (hyper-CSE). An extreme positive self-assessment can lead these builders to overestimate their ability to manage risk, underestimate the capital required to launch new (read: risky) initiatives, and underestimate the uncertainties or potential perils in the external business or nonprofit environment.

If you are a hyper-confident builder, you are certain that you can do no wrong and that you can resolve all problems if a decision turns bad. You are likely to engage in impulsive or uninformed risk-taking, are less accurate in your forecast of success, and are more likely to persist in pursuing strategies even when they are not delivering the results you hoped for. In addition, hyper-CSE may lead to "shiny new object syndrome" — when you invest in multiple projects, overestimating your ability to get positive results from all of them, and in the process, end up hurting your core business — or your organization's main mission and purpose.

Make sure to evaluate an opportunity rationally and thoroughly before taking action. Get feedback from people in your circle of trust. Take your time deciding which projects build on your core business — or your organization's mission and purpose — and which are likely to take you off course. Keep the former, and get rid of the latter.

Risk Talent in Action:

Bill Gates on Warren Buffett: "Warren doesn't outperform other investors because he computes odds better. That's not it at all. Warren never makes an investment where the difference between doing it and not doing it relies on the second digit of computation. He doesn't invest — take a swing of the bat — unless the opportunity appears unbelievably good."

Jeff Bezos, founder and CEO of Amazon.com: "Ninety-plus percent of the innovation at Amazon is incremental and critical and much less risky. We know how to open new product categories. We know how to open new geographies. That doesn't mean that these things are guaranteed to work, but we have a lot of expertise and a lot of knowledge. All of these things based on our operating history are things that we can analyze quantitatively rather than to have to make intuitive judgments."

Andy Dunn, co-founder and CEO of Bonobos: "Prior to a lobotomy I just underwent which removed shiny new object syndrome (SNOS) from my brain, I was both an asset and a threat to my own company. The company is trying to do one thing, and I would come up with another. I can't tell you how dangerous this is. If the founder doesn't know what the company is doing, the company won't either."

Maximizing Your Risk Talent:

1. *Know what you do know and what you do not know.* Understand the limits of your knowledge. Recognize the preferences and biases inherent in your worldview that can affect your judgment about the results you expect. Resist predicting outcomes based on limited evidence. Gather all relevant information before you take action.

2. *Take risks incrementally.* When exploring a new venture, a new market or a new product, minimize risks by making a small initial investment and evaluating the idea at successive stages in the development process. Consider it an experiment. Build a prototype, test the market and collect information. Then decide if the idea is worth investing in further or abandoning.

3. *Beware of confirmation bias.* Your extremely positive self-image may lead you to favor information that confirms your beliefs and opinions, while discounting information that contradicts your viewpoint. Do not let this bias influence your decision-making. Ask people with opposing views to counter your initial idea or concept. Considering different points of view as well as your own will help you perceive opportunities more realistically and pick the ones with a higher probability of success.

4. *Construct different scenarios to guide your decision-making process.* Envision how things will unfold in the future, analyze the different directions a project can take and estimate the outcomes in all directions. When you bring potential risk factors to light, you can choose the least risky path.

5. *Don't gamble.* Take careful calculated risks. Before an exciting idea sweeps you away in anticipation of what you will accomplish, impose a cooling-off period of a few weeks before you commit any funds. This will give you time to calculate the odds of success and put a plan in place to mitigate the risks.

6. *Kill unimportant projects.* You might overestimate your ability to succeed at multiple projects simultaneously. With your team, analyze all the projects in your organization. Keep your focus on projects that strengthen and build on your organization's core business or mission and purpose. Ditch the rest.

SELLING

Key Traits:

- You speak boldly on behalf of your organization.

- You make your case effectively and influence people.

- You communicate your vision of your organization to employees and customers.

- You have a clear growth strategy.

Highly successful builders are ambassadors who represent the interests of their organization to the outside world. If you have high Selling talent, you are the face and voice of your organization. At every opportunity, you champion its mission and purpose and endorse what it stands for.

As someone with high Selling talent, you are an excellent communicator who instinctively knows how to reach your audience. Incredibly persuasive, you are a great salesperson who can influence others to accept your point of view. Your open and authentic behavior helps you forge trusting relationships with investors, customers, partners and employees that help you launch new products and services to grow your organization.

Builders with high Selling talent are exceptional storytellers. You communicate the essence of your organization, your idea, or your new product or service through stories that reflect your personal experiences. You create an emotional connection with your audience by sharing your passion and excitement about the product or service, but also by speaking to your listeners' needs. Your storytelling helps rally support for your cause from your partners and customers and furthers your organizational goals.

As an attentive listener, you are quick to assess customer or societal needs and can clearly and compellingly articulate how your product, service or mission will meet those needs. Your unbridled enthusiasm and deep conviction in your product or service inspires trust and persuades your prospects to say yes. You establish your credibility by being forthright and sharing facts. This reassures your clients and builds long-term customer commitment.

You instinctively know how to invest in people and relationships that are beneficial to your organization. You form close connections with employees so they feel emotionally invested in their work, with investors or donors to secure financial resources you need to grow, with vendors who get emotionally attached to your product or mission, and with customers to turn them into evangelists. You can cultivate a community of supporters who become ambassadors for your product, service or mission.

A word of caution: Highly successful builders with dominant Selling talent have a natural tendency to believe that their organization, product, service or mission has the potential to change the world. Your closeness to your idea or product and an intense desire to see it succeed may blind you to its flaws. While storytelling and advocacy are critical to growing an organization, be objective about the product or service you promote. Surround yourself with trusted advisers who will help you assess situations and scenarios objectively. Take the time to build something that will truly solve someone's organizational or societal problem. Promoting a solid product or service builds customer trust and long-term commitment.

In addition, even though you like to be the face of your organization, consider if that is always in the enterprise's best interest. Sure, when a builder writes syndicated columns or blogs, appears in the media, and gives speeches, it can give an organization a distinct identity and help it grow. But creating a single dominant persona that represents the organization may be counterproductive for organizations that need to emphasize the availability of diverse expert resources for the customer. And the reality is, an organization that is built around the personality of its founder or owner may find it hard to convince customers to work with anyone else, potentially restricting its growth. Sometimes, it is better to present multiple faces and voices of your organization.

Selling Talent in Action:

David Ogilvy, founder of Ogilvy & Mather and known as "The Father of Advertising": "In the modern world of business, it is useless to be a creative, original thinker unless you can also sell what you create."

Peter Guber, chairman and CEO of Mandalay Entertainment Group: "My experience at Sony demonstrated that the face-to-face telling of the right story in the right room at the right time and in the right way can galvanize listeners to action and reset the teller's success trajectory."

Dino Bernacchi, former director of North American marketing operations for Harley-Davidson: "*United by Independents* is as much a rally cry to discover your ultimate self-expression and personal freedom as it is a celebration of fans and riders that continue to defy stereotypes of what it means to be a Harley-Davidson enthusiast. The campaign is cast entirely through social media with real riders from across the globe and from all walks of life who are united by their shared passion for the brand and their love of riding."

Maximizing Your Selling Talent:

1. *Build a great product or service.* Make sure to anticipate your customers' needs as you create your product or service. Shrewdly designed products and services empower customers and are easy to build a brand around and promote.

2. *Be the expert.* Position yourself as the expert on your organization's products and services. Blog, speak and write about the value they bring to your customers. Use your natural storytelling talent to elaborate on how your products or services are different from the sea of competition out there. The information you offer will establish you as the expert your customers can trust.

3. *Rehearse your stories.* Take every opportunity to practice your storytelling technique. Refine each story based on your audience's feedback. Go beyond your personal experiences and add anecdotes from history, mythology, politics and literature. Create a message that helps you achieve your organization's goals.

4. *Use multiple media to reach the widest audience possible.* In addition to traditional means of communication, make the most of media such as Twitter, Facebook, texting and blogging. The more accessible you are, the more seeds you plant.

5. *Build and support a community for your products and services.* Your organization can benefit greatly from customers who love your product or service. Identify them, and help them champion your offerings. Provide them with the latest information on your product or service, give them a forum to share their views, use their feedback to improve your product or service, share their stories on your organization's website, and give them physical space to hold meetings and interact with your employees. In short, create a community of evangelists for your organization.

APPENDIX

TOOLS AND RESOURCES

Launching and building a venture is a challenging task. So Gallup created several tools and resources to help you get started. These tools will guide you through the process of creating self-awareness, developing a network, recognizing and assessing opportunities, building and testing your minimally viable product or service with customers, and forming highly productive teams.

Use these tools to set specific goals for each stage of your journey and to track your progress. Setting goals and keeping track will make you mindful of the actions you are taking (or not taking) and build accountability — and will be the key to your success.

You will be able to download full, editable versions of each of these tools from our website after you take the BP10 assessment. To take the assessment, you will need the unique access code in the packet at the back of the book. See the next few pages for thumbnails and brief descriptions of the tools for your reference.

We hope that these tools are useful on your journey.

Self-Schema Tool

Create an internal map of your personal characteristics to better understand your talents, behaviors and worldview.

The First Key: Creating Self-Awareness

Board of Directors Tool

Identify the members of your personal board of directors, and determine what you need from each one: the role they play, how often you need to interact, how close you are and what type of support you need.

The First Key: Creating Self-Awareness

Purpose Journal Tool

Keep track of your positive experiences, plans for the future and interactions with board members to build self-awareness and create a record of your successes (or failures).

The First Key: Creating Self-Awareness

Opportunity Journal Tool

Start identifying the opportunities around you by recording your daily activities and tasks and then rating your level of engagement, learning curve and performance for each one.

The Second Key:
Recognizing Opportunities

Storyboard Tool

Analyze the viability of your ideas by defining your purpose, product or service, customer needs, value add, resources, affordable loss, and success.

The Second Key:
Recognizing Opportunities

Activation Chart Tool

Refine your product or service using the cycle of generating and testing hypotheses, learning from your experiments, and applying what you learn.

The Third Key: Activating on Ideas

Team Talent Map Tool

Map the talents of current or potential team members, and clarify your team's roles, strengths and potential talent gaps.

The Fourth Key: Building a Team

Extended Team Tool

Develop a broad and diverse network by exploring your personal relationships to identify who can connect you to people, expertise and resources that will fulfill your venture's needs and help you reach your overall goals.

The Fourth Key: Building a Team

BUSINESS OUTCOMES

Gallup research indicates that each builder talent is highly relevant to specific business outcomes. In a logistic regression analysis, we found relationships between psychological contexts and business outcomes.

Gallup asked entrepreneurs the following questions about their revenue; growth goals; how many businesses they have started; plans for growing their employee base; and their copyright, trademark and patent ownership.

Q1. What is the current revenue in your most recent business? (in U.S. dollars)

- a) Less than $50,000
- b) $50,000 to less than $250,000
- c) $250,000 to less than $500,000
- d) $500,000 to less than $1 million
- e) $1 million to less than $5 million
- f) $5 million to less than $10 million
- g) $10 million to less than $50 million
- h) $50 million to less than $100 million
- i) $100 million and above

Q2. Thinking ahead to the next five years, which of the following best describes your revenue goals for your business?

    a) I want to shrink the size of my business

    b) I want to maintain the size of my business

    c) I want to moderately grow the size of my business

    d) I want to significantly grow the size of my business

Q3. How many businesses have you started, regardless of whether they are still in operation?

    a) 1

    b) 2

    c) 3

    d) 4

    e) 5 or more

Q4. In the next 12 months, by what percentage do you expect to increase the number of employees?

    a) Plan to decrease number of employees

    b) No change in number of employees

    c) Increase by less than 5%

    d) Increase 5%-10%

    e) Increase more than 10%

Q5. Does your current business own one or more of the following?

    a) Copyright

    b) Trademark

    c) Patent (granted)

    d) Patent pending

Each variable was recoded to create performance categories relevant to a business that is sustainable and growing. For instance, *Revenue* (Q1) was collapsed into a new variable containing revenue categories of less than $1 million and more than $1 million. We selected the cutoff of $1 million in revenue, as businesses that reach the $1 million mark are considered sustainable, with a high likelihood of growth. Similarly, the new variable captures *Growth* by collapsing Q2 into those who want to *grow significantly* versus all others. The indicator for *Serial Entrepreneur* was obtained by collapsing Q3 into those who started three or more businesses versus those with fewer than three businesses. The indicator for *Job Creation* was derived by collapsing Q4 into those hiring more than 5% versus others. Finally, the indicator for *Innovation* was derived by collapsing Q5 into those who have patent(s) granted or pending versus all others.

BUILDER PROFILE 10
METHODOLOGY REPORT

INTRODUCTION

Gallup developed the Builder Profile 10 (BP10) to assess an individual's entrepreneurial talent. Extending across disciplinary boundaries of economics, psychology and management, Gallup researchers wanted to understand entrepreneurship's psychological roots.

Scientists at Gallup developed the BP10 assessment based on qualitative and quantitative research using professional standards (i.e., American Educational Research Association/American Psychological Association/National Council on Measurement in Education, 1999; Society for Industrial and Organizational Psychology, 2003) and the Uniform Guidelines on Employee Selection Procedures. The result of Gallup's research and development was a structured, web-based assessment designed to assess the talents needed for success in entrepreneurial activities. This report describes the development of the BP10 assessment and provides validity evidence to support its proper applications.

PSYCHOLOGY OF ENTREPRENEURSHIP: REVIEW OF THE RESEARCH

Personality research in industrial and organizational psychology has long tied personality variables to organizational (Hunter, 1986; Barrick & Mount, 1991) and leadership performance (Judge, Bono, Ilies & Gerhardt, 2002). Many researchers define personality traits as enduring dispositions that are relatively stable over time and across situations (Rauch & Frese, 2007). In the realm of entrepreneurship, traits explain entrepreneurial behavior. Numerous studies show that entrepreneurial attitudes toward autonomy, risk, work and income are more important than factors such as access to credit or location in determining the success of a firm (Davidsson & Honig, 2003; Dimov & Shepherd, 2005; Duchesneau & Gartner, 1990; Haber & Reichel, 2007; Lerner & Haber, 2001; Shaw & Williams, 1998). In other words, an individual's unique traits can influence their ability to recognize a business opportunity and act to make the most of that opportunity in ways that others cannot (Badal, 2010). So what are the characteristics that drive an individual to business creation under great resource scarcity and high uncertainty? How do these characteristics affect the entrepreneur's decision-making process leading to venture creation and success or failure? The answers lie in understanding the inherent traits that influence behaviors driving business creation and success.

Researchers have identified numerous traits, such as risk propensity (Arenius & Minniti, 2005; Engle, Mah & Sadri, 1997; Smith-Hunter, Kapp & Yonkers, 2003; Stewart & Roth, 2004), creativity (Engle, Mah & Sadri, 1997), problem-solving and overcoming obstacles (Morris, Avila & Allen, 1993; Smith-Hunter, Kapp & Yonkers, 2003), achievement orientation (Collins, Hanges & Locke, 2004; Smith-Hunter, Kapp & Yonkers, 2003), self-efficacy (Arenius & Minniti, 2005; Chen, Greene & Crick, 1998), and high sense of responsibility (Smith-Hunter, Kapp & Yonkers, 2003), as key charactristics of a successful entrepreneur. In addition, behavioral economists consider bounded rationality (Simon, Houghton & Aquino, 1999), inherent biases in probability perception (Kunreuther et al., 2002) and biases in self-perception (Koellinger, Minniti & Schade, 2007; Minniti & Nardone, 2007; Hoelzl & Rustichini, 2005) as significant factors affecting an entrepreneur's decision-making process, which ultimately affects business outcomes.

Gallup research indicates that an individual's inherent talent for a role — one's natural capacity for excellence in a role — results in greater efficiency and productivity in that activity and provides a more fulfilling experience for the individual. Talent is a broader concept than personality traits. Talent is a composite of innate personality traits, attitudes, motives, cognition and values. Using selection science, Gallup researchers could determine if a candidate possesses a critical mass of talent relative to the typical characteristics of the most successful people in a given role and predict whether that candidate was more likely to naturally and consistently behave in ways that lead to excellence in the role. Certain patterns are dominant and become salient descriptors of a person's approach to everyday experiences, including work. Consequently, these talents offer the greatest area for potential growth (Clifton & Nelson, 1992). These talents can be used to understand people and predict their behaviors in a particular context.

A major component of Gallup's efforts involves identifying and studying patterns of excellence among successful people. This study focuses on recurring and consistent patterns of thought, feeling or behavior of successful entrepreneurs — manifestations that consistently occur when talented entrepreneurs are exposed to specific stimuli. Through Gallup researchers' more than 40 years of qualitative and quantitative research, it was determined that, when objectively assessed, successful people respond differently than less successful people. The development of the BP10 Index used this cumulative experience and knowledge. Gallup used its database and senior researchers' experience and expertise to develop a pilot selection assessment with the potential to understand the patterns of excellence that characterize outstanding entrepreneurs.

PART I: INSTRUMENT DEVELOPMENT PROCESS

Theoretical Considerations

The conceptual foundation on which Gallup researchers built the final BP10 Index begins with delineating the demands of the role and the desirable behavioral responses to meet such demands and hypothesizing the talents that enable those desirable behavioral responses that lead to entrepreneurial success. An adaptation of the Giessen-Amsterdam model (Rauch & Frese, 2000) appears below and shows the link between individual differences and entrepreneurial performance.

Builder Profile 10: Pathways From Talent to Business Success

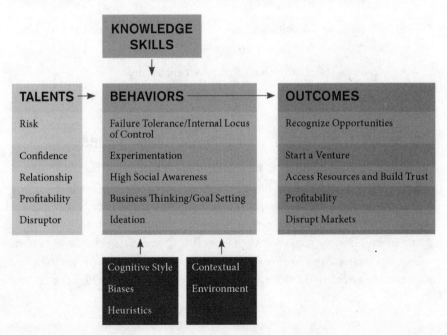

This modified model shows how talents affect key behaviors that enable an entrepreneur to meet the demands of the job and ultimately lead to business creation or success. Thus, the talent-based assessment solutions predictive of successful performance in the role are those that effectively capture the talents that could enable the key behaviors. Many other factors also play a role in determining entrepreneurial performance, such as knowledge/skills, cognitive styles, biases and several contextual factors (industry type, life stage, economic and political environment, access to credit, and others), but this report focuses on an entrepreneur's innate talents and their relationship to business outcomes.

Following the model previously mentioned, the development of a talent-based assessment begins with the study of a role and the successful incumbents in that role. These two interrelated topics become the focal point of the qualitative research. Specifically, the qualitative research intends to:

- define the target roles by describing the demands they place on the individuals in the role

- delineate the behavioral responses needed to meet the demands of the role

- differentiate the behavioral responses according to the extent that they meet the job demands, from low to high

- derive the talent constructs that might enable those behavioral responses

Overview of the Instrument Development Process

The foundation for building the BP10 assessment began in the late 1980s, when Gallup researchers developed a framework for the process of new venture creation and studied the psychological factors that drive successful entrepreneurship (SRI/ Gallup, 1989). In 2008, Gallup collaborated with NaturTalent Stiftung in Baden-Wurttemberg, Germany, to study the talents that differentiate entrepreneurs from non-entrepreneurs (von, Dabiri & Truscott-Smith, 2009). Learnings from the qualitative research conducted in 1989 and 2008 led to the development of the current BP10 assessment. The present BP10 assessment further extends the talent model to differentiate successful entrepreneurs from less successful ones.

The development of the BP10 assessment involved the following steps:

1. Conduct qualitative research.

2. Design and administer the pilot study.

3. Analyze the data and develop the final assessment.

Conduct Qualitative Research

The qualitative research provided initial evidence regarding the content relevance of the BP10 assessment to the entrepreneurial role. Gallup researchers conducted systematic investigations of high-performing entrepreneurs in a study of U.S. entrepreneurs in 1989 and in a study of German entrepreneurs in Baden-Wurttemberg, Germany, in 2008. Researchers conducted stakeholder interviews and focus groups with existing entrepreneurs who had successful company operations. With participants' agreement, researchers recorded all interviews and focus groups (conducted face to face or via telephone). Participants in these discussions answered many questions about the functions they routinely perform. Researchers paid particular attention to the attitudes and behaviors that outstanding entrepreneurs exhibited and used information collected through the discussions to identify the talents that enable success in an entrepreneurial role. The research led to a description of the role, the job demands and the initial talent model.

In 2009, Gallup researchers conducted a comprehensive literature review that led to the further refinement of the talent model and development of the current BP10 instrument. Researchers identified additional constructs to differentiate a successful entrepreneur from a less successful one. To ensure the content appropriateness of the BP10 assessment to the role of a successful entrepreneur, Gallup researchers used information gathered through stakeholder interviews and focus groups in Nebraska and Germany and the extensive literature review. The goal of the BP10 assessment is to identify entrepreneurs who are likely to significantly grow their business.

Findings From the Qualitative Research

The Target Role

An "entrepreneur" is someone who builds economic value by creating products and services for the market. Following Timmons' (1994) conception of entrepreneurship as the "process of creating or seizing an opportunity and pursuing it," Gallup researchers focused on entrepreneurs who are driven to fulfill a gap in the market rather than starting businesses to make ends meet. Though the reasons for starting a business can be complex, Bogenhold (1987) differentiated "opportunity-driven" entrepreneurs, who are motivated to enter entrepreneurship more out of choice to exploit an opportunity, from "necessity-driven" entrepreneurs, who are pushed into entrepreneurial activity in the absence of other options for work. Studies show that opportunity-driven entrepreneurs differ from their necessity-driven counterparts in their entrepreneurial behaviors and growth aspirations and business growth (Acs, Desai & Hessels, 2008). Because opportunity-driven entrepreneurs expect higher growth and create more jobs (Acs et al., 2008), Gallup researchers focused on the individuals engaged in the more desirable opportunity-driven entrepreneurship rather than the necessity-induced entrepreneurship.

To accomplish their objective of creating goods and services for the market, entrepreneurs must engage in various tasks or activities to start and subsequently grow a business. The phases of business setup: 1) recognizing opportunities that arise because of changing economic, social or technological conditions; 2) pursuing these opportunities proactively; 3) gathering human and financial resources that enable a startup; 4) creating a road map or a strategy to produce a product or service; 5) launching a new venture; and finally, 6) actively managing the company (Shane, 2003; Bygrave, 1989).

Each phase of the entrepreneurial process requires that the entrepreneur perform specific activities. For instance, in the early stages, recognizing opportunities leads to evaluating these opportunities, thinking through all the possibilities and practicalities, and leveraging relationships to find partnerships to launch a venture. After establishing the company, actively managing the company means the entrepreneur must oversee a workforce, influence and motivate others, and conduct negotiations with customers or suppliers (Baron, 2006).

The study of the entrepreneur's role revealed that successful entrepreneurs exhibited various behaviors allowing them to meet the needs of the role at

174

each stage of the business. Table 1 provides a list of the behaviors successful entrepreneurs exhibit and the underlying talents that drive the behaviors that ultimately result in business creation and success. Though the table below matches a specific talent to a set of behaviors, in reality, multiple talents can drive a behavior. The table lists the talents that are dominant in driving specific behaviors.

Table 1: Entrepreneurial Behaviors and Talents

Behaviors That Enable Entrepreneurs to Meet the Demands of the Role	Talents That Drive the Behaviors
<ul><li>Know themselves and present themselves effectively and with confidence — even in the face of rejection</li><li>Clearly understand others</li><li>Build trust and invest in people</li><li>Able to articulate the competitive advantage of their firm in the marketplace</li><li>Align employee activities with their individual strengths, leading to business growth</li></ul>	Confidence
<ul><li>Show a strong personality and are charismatic and confident</li><li>Show enthusiasm and emotion in taking on challenges</li><li>Have highly optimistic perception of risk</li><li>Can easily make decisions in complex situations</li><li>Can easily establish emotional connections with customers, are more likely to understand what customers need, share new ideas with customers and are more likely to exceed customer expectations</li></ul>	Risk
<ul><li>Imagine beyond the boundaries of what exists now</li><li>Explore options and can think their way through problems</li><li>Are constantly thinking of creating new products and/or services for their customers</li><li>Have minds that are typically firing with many different ideas</li><li>Are curious and quick learners</li></ul>	Disruptor

Table 1: Entrepreneurial Behaviors and Talents

Behaviors That Enable Entrepreneurs to Meet the Demands of the Role	Talents That Drive the Behaviors
• Have a clear, strong voice and speak boldly on behalf of their company • Have the ability to make their case effectively and have others follow their decisions • Communicate their vision of their company to employees and customers • Have a clear growth strategy	Selling
• Are profit-oriented • Establish clear goals and objectively measure their progress toward the goal • Judge the value of an opportunity, a relationship or a decision by its effect on business • Invest time in planning growth strategies • Align employee responsibilities with company goals	Profitability
• Seek knowledge that is relevant to growing their business • Push themselves to acquire in-depth information about every aspect of their business • Have a preoccupation with their business that borders on obsession • Anticipate knowledge needs and use knowledge well	Knowledge
• Depend on themselves to get the job done • Have a strong sense of responsibility • Can handle multiple tasks successfully • Are resolute, with a high level of competence in every aspect of managing a business	Independence

Table 1: Entrepreneurial Behaviors and Talents

Behaviors That Enable Entrepreneurs to Meet the Demands of the Role	Talents That Drive the Behaviors
<ul><li>Push to achieve more and have a tremendous work ethic</li><li>Instigate the action to get something started</li><li>Are eager to make decisions and quick to act</li><li>Confront obstacles directly and overcome them</li><li>Are persistent and undeterred by failure and/or roadblocks</li></ul>	Determination
<ul><li>Understand that they cannot do everything themselves if the business is going to expand</li><li>Can readily delegate authority and responsibility</li><li>Can proactively collaborate with others</li><li>Recognize and draw on people's special abilities</li><li>Help ensure that team members become effective contributors to the company</li></ul>	Delegator
<ul><li>Have high social awareness</li><li>Can attract and maintain a constituency</li><li>Build mutually beneficial relationships</li><li>Use their relationship talents to access internal and external resources</li><li>Forge relationships with employees and customers that go beyond work or products or services</li><li>Have an open demeanor, positive attitude and personal integrity that helps build trust</li></ul>	Relationship

The 10 talents described in Table 1 influence behaviors that best explain success in an entrepreneurial role. An individual's inherent talents and acquired ability (skills, knowledge and experience) influence how successfully and by what means they respond to the needs of the role. The individual's dispositions or talents enable appropriate behavioral responses. Typically, the more prevalent the talent, the higher the likelihood of success in the role.

Design and Administer the Pilot Study

Using a talent-based description of a successful entrepreneur, Gallup researchers created an online (web-based) interview to assess the existence of the attributes listed in the talent model. The pilot assessment included 113 items. Researchers selected a combination of multiple-choice and Likert items based on their content relevance and statistical properties indicated by item histories. The items came from the Gallup Item Bank. The Item Bank contains more than 9,000 items of different types that Gallup has used previously. Many of these items tap into entrepreneurial talents specifically. An item history includes information about each item's performance with past research participants, including statistics on item characteristics; relationships between item responses and performance measures; and relationships between item responses and race, gender and age variables.

In addition, Gallup researchers included a series of questions about participants' business backgrounds and demographics to ensure that those whom Gallup classified as successful entrepreneurs were correctly assigned to each group. These questions asked about the number of businesses participants had started, business successes and failures they may have had, number of employees, profit, sales goals, and expectations of business performance in the future.

Gallup invited 1,736 self-employed Gallup Panel members (a probability-based, nationally representative panel of U.S. households) to participate in the web-based pilot study to test the existence of the hypothetical talents and build the instrument. Of these Panel members, 1,188 identified themselves as "primary owners" of a business and provided valid responses to enough items for Gallup to use in the research sample.

Gallup researchers focused their attention on opportunity-driven entrepreneurs. These entrepreneurs identified "good startup opportunities in my area," "opportunity to be independent" or "opportunity to increase my income" as their main reason for starting a business. Of the 1,188 primary owners, 905 were opportunity-driven entrepreneurs based on their reason for starting a business. Researchers labeled respondents who gave their reason for starting a business as "no jobs available in my area" as necessity-based entrepreneurs and excluded them from the sample.

Analyze the Data and Develop the Final Assessment

Gallup researchers used the data gathered from the pilot assessment to evaluate the psychometric properties of each item and the assessment as a whole. This evaluation included, among others, analyses on:

- appropriateness of each item, and the assessment as a whole, as representation of the talents identified as important

- item characteristics such as item difficulty

- relationships between item responses and total scores and the performance variable

- relationships between item responses and demographic variables

- reliability of the total score

Conducting descriptive and inferential analyses, Gallup researchers studied which items best differentiated top-performing entrepreneurs from others. In addition to prior research, these analyses provided basis for questions retained for the field study. The field instrument contained 89 items that best cover the common talents needed for achieving high levels of success in starting or growing businesses. Researchers calculated the Index Total Score using these items. The score is an integer between zero and 100 that indicates the percentage of points an individual received out of the total possible points. Higher scores indicate potentially better performance in the entrepreneurial role. In addition, various demographic items, 42 non-scored research items and nine contextual items that assess the environment in which the entrepreneur exists are also included. The research and contextual items will allow for adjustments to the assessment in the future to enhance its efficiency and utility. As such, the assessment has a degree of flexibility, while maintaining the core foundational elements for estimating entrepreneurial talent. The assessment takes the average respondent 25 to 30 minutes to complete.

Overview of Validity Evidence

Validity is the degree to which both theory and empirical evidence support inferences and actions based on an assessment. Validation is an ongoing process of developing sound arguments and gathering evidence that supports the intended interpretation and actions based on the assessment outcome. Validity evidence may be derived from empirical data, relevant literature, expert judgments and logical analysis.

Support for the Use of Talent-Based Structured Assessments

Published Meta-Analyses

The research exploring linkages between broad and specific traits to business performance has shown contradictory results. For instance, Brandstatter (1997) did not find any differences in broad traits between business owners and non-owners but did find a positive link between emotional stability, independence and entrepreneurial success. On the other hand, Wooten and Timmerman (1999) found that openness to experience was negatively related to business startup. Another study (Ciaverella, Bucholtz, Riordan, Gatewood & Stokes, 2004) found a negative relationship between openness to experience and business survival but a positive relationship between conscientiousness and business survival. Despite contradictory results in individual studies, a meta-analysis by Rauch and Frese (2007) showed that both broad (r = 0.151) and specific traits (r = 0.231) had a significant relationship to entrepreneurial success. Following this line of research, Gallup researchers developed the current BP10 assessment to usefully differentiate entrepreneurs from non-entrepreneurs.

Gallup Meta-Analyses

Schmidt and Rader (1999) conducted a meta-analysis of 107 of Gallup's predictive validity studies and found that the type of structured interview process Gallup researchers used (the in-depth interview) results in scores that are predictive of multiple performance criteria, including sales data, production records, absenteeism and employee retention. A more recent meta-analysis of Gallup selection assessments (based on 386 predictive validity studies and expanded to interactive voice response and web modes) again indicated that Gallup's selection assessment methodology produced positive and generalizable predictive validity across various criterion types and positions (Harter, Hayes & Schmidt, 2004). The BP10 is a structured web assessment developed using the same methodology and is expected to be predictive of specific performance criteria such as sales and profit growth.

Analyses and Results From the Pilot Sample

Sample

A total of 1,188 self-employed people from the Gallup Panel completed the research assessment. As explained previously, Gallup designated 905 of these people as opportunity-based entrepreneurs based on their responses to their reason for starting a business. Researchers identified the research sample to represent entrepreneurs who performed at low, average and high levels. The performance groups in the sample, so formed, are referred to as contrast, middle and study groups hereafter. The designations of the performance groups used a composite performance rating developed by combining several outcome variables.

Table 2 shows the number of entrepreneurs in the sample by performance category.

Table 2: Sample of Opportunity-Based Entrepreneurs

All Invitees	Total # of Opportunity-Based Entrepreneurs	Sample by Performance			
		Total	Contrast	Middle	Study
1,188	905	905	301	302	302

The companies in the analysis had been in existence from less than 10 years to more than 50 years (by 2009). Table 3 shows the distribution of businesses by start year.

Table 3: Distribution of Businesses by Start Year

Year Business Started	In Sample	Percentage
1959 or prior	2	0.2%
1960-1969	16	1.8%
1970-1979	46	5.1%
1980-1989	141	15.6%
1990-1999	244	27.0%
2000-2009	456	50.4%
Total	905	100%

Table 4 shows sample sizes broken out by race, gender and age. All research participants completed the assessment in U.S. English.

Table 4: Demographics

Variable	In Sample
Race	
White (not Hispanic or Latino)	825
All nonwhite (not Hispanic or Latino)	70
Black (not Hispanic or Latino)	13
Hispanic or Latino	0
Native American (not Hispanic or Latino)	22
Asian (not Hispanic or Latino)	7
Pacific Islander (not Hispanic or Latino)	3
Other	25
Missing race information	10
Gender	
Male	539
Female	366
Age	
Younger than 40	92
40 and older	759
Missing age information	54

Reliability of the Index Score

Reliability, in the context of measurement, refers to the degree of consistency and stability of outcomes produced by a measurement process (e.g., a selection assessment administered via the web) across the replications of some aspects of the process. There are many types of reliability indexes; each characterizes somewhat different aspects of error in a measurement process. The magnitude of different aspects of measurement errors can be described by the standard error of measurement (SEM), which directly relates to the magnitude of the reliability coefficient of the corresponding type.

Internal Consistency Reliability

The assessment development study allows for evaluation of the internal consistency reliability. A higher degree of internal consistency is desirable because it indicates an assessment is able to obtain consistent responses from the respondents. Gallup's minimum standard for total score reliability on its assessments is 0.70. Table 5 reports the internal consistency reliability (Cronbach's alpha coefficient) of the BP10 assessment.

Table 5: Reliability and Descriptive Statistics for BP10 Assessment

Index	Number of Items	a	Mean	SD	SEM
BP10	89	0.90	58.02	9.59	3.03

Note:
a = Cronbach's alpha
SD = standard deviation
SEM = standard error of measurement

Identifying the Talent Themes: Factor Analyses

In addition to the Total Index Score, which is indicative of overall entrepreneurial potential, researchers conducted factor analysis to parse items into talent themes. Researchers used principal components analysis because the primary purpose was to identify and calculate composite scores for the talent themes underlying the BP10 assessment.

Researchers defined a-priori 10-factor structure based on theoretical support for talents entrepreneurs need to be successful in the role. Using varimax and oblimin rotations of the factor-loading matrix, researchers examined solutions for 10 factors. Results of both methods were similar. The 10-factor structure explained 41% of the variance. Items with a factor loading of 0.30 or above on a factor were retained. To label the factors in the model, researchers examined the factor pattern to see which items loaded highly (0.30 or above) on which factors and then determined the common theme of the items. For the most part, the items loaded on the correct factors (all nine Confidence items loaded together on a single factor, all Risk items loaded together on a single factor and so on), thus confirming that the analysis produced the correct factor structure. Researchers made minor adjustments where items did not load on the expected factors. In sum, the conceptual talent model created by the researchers closely matched the results of the principal component analysis (PCA), indicating that the correct conclusions regarding the underlying factor structure for those items have been attained by the PCA.

All factors except Delegator have five or more strongly loading items (0.40 or better), indicating a solid factor. Researchers examined internal consistency for each of the themes using Cronbach's alpha. The alphas were moderate: all above 0.50 except Delegator ($a = 0.32$). No substantial increases in alpha for any of the themes could have been achieved by eliminating more items. Individual themes are not intended as independent predictors of entrepreneurial success. The primary use of individual theme measurement is for developmental purposes.

Next, researchers created composite scores for each of the 10 talent themes based on the mean of the items that had their primary loadings on each factor. Higher scores on the theme indicated greater likelihood of success in meeting a specific need of the role.

The talent themes of entrepreneurship represent what an entrepreneur needs to do to be successful in starting or growing a business. While the themes are comprehensive, they are not intended as predictors of entrepreneurial success individually. Continuing research will focus on strengthening each of the themes through revision (rewriting) items with lower primary loadings and possibly adding new items. In addition, confirmatory factor analysis, as well as other latent variable modeling techniques, will also be used to further refine the thematic structure.

Table 6: Reliability and Descriptive Statistics for Talent Theme Scores

Talent Themes	Number of Items	a	Mean	SD
Confidence	9	0.74	65.22	11.69
Risk	12	0.67	50.85	11.48
Disruptor	9	0.67	63.58	14.41
Selling	8	0.60	56.27	16.91
Profitability	6	0.50	51.80	20.03
Knowledge	6	0.47	66.49	14.52
Independence	10	0.60	54.49	14.29
Determination	14	0.69	69.57	13.57
Delegator	4	0.32	24.53	24.11
Relationship	12	0.69	57.79	15.82

Note:
a = Cronbach's alpha
SD = standard deviation

Test-Retest Reliability

Test-retest reliability indicates the stability of assessment outcomes over time and across occasions. Although Gallup could not collect such evidence with the current study, researchers' analyses on similar assessments generally show a high degree of test-retest reliability. A Gallup study on web-based assessments involving different samples and assessments reported a sample-size-weighted average test-retest reliability of 0.81 (Harter, 2003). It should also be pointed out that the BP10 Index measures talent constructs that have high trait composition. Thus, they are expected to be relatively stable over the course of one's lifespan.

Concurrent Criterion-Related Validity Evidence

Criterion-related validity evidence indicates the extent to which assessment outcomes are predictive of individual performance in specified activities. Gallup gathers criterion-related validity evidence by examining the relationships between its assessment outcomes and measures that adequately reflect performance in the role. Researchers can use both concurrent and predictive designs to gather such evidence.

Gallup collects concurrent criterion-related validity evidence from assessment development studies, such as the one described in this report. In these studies, researchers collect outcomes on assessment and performance data from existing entrepreneurs at approximately the same time. Concurrent studies allow for demonstrations of desirable relationships between assessment outcomes and performance in the role. Such relationships further support the role-relatedness and business relevance of the assessment outcomes.

Properties of Performance Measure

In criterion-related validity analysis, the quality of performance measures researchers use as criteria is vital. The appropriateness and quality of performance measures may be evaluated with respect to the extent that they:

- are aligned with the key demands of the role
- have crucial implications to business outcomes
- reflect the definitions of various performance levels

- have clear definition and calculation/process/rubric
- can be attributable to the individual being measured
- are resistant to biasing factors in the measurement process
- are reliable across measurement occasions
- produce reasonable variance to effectively separate various performance levels
- are accessible and can be obtained with reasonable data collection time/efforts

The key criterion measure used in the analysis was a composite of nine questions that capture the entrepreneur's current profit and sales performance (Q04-Q09), future expectations (Q01) and job creation potential (Q02 and Q03). Gallup researchers used self-reported profit and sales performance to capture performance because collecting objective metrics from a large sample of entrepreneurs was not practical. To provide a more stable measure of the various business outcomes, researchers formed a composite with unit-weighted z scores of constituent variables (Ackerman & Cianciolo, 2000). The group designations — study, middle, contrast — were based on the tri-tiles of the composite score.

Q01. In the next five years, I expect profit to be a) very high, b) moderate to good, c) poor to fair.

Q02. Has the number of employees in your most recent business a) increased, b) decreased, or c) remained about the same since you started your business?

Q03. I expect to create a minimum of _____ additional jobs in the next five years.

Q04. How did your most recent business perform relative to profit goals for 2008?

Q05. How did your most recent business perform relative to profit goals for 2007?

Q06. How did your most recent business perform relative to profit goals for 2006?

Q07. How did your most recent business perform relative to sales goals for 2008?

Q08. How did your most recent business perform relative to sales goals for 2007?

Q09. How did your most recent business perform relative to sales goals for 2006?

The composite score has values between -1.41 and 2.00. Correlation between the grouping variable and the performance composite score is 0.89 and statistically significant at 0.01 level. This indicates that those designated in the study group had better performance in the role than those in the middle group, and those in the middle had better performance than those in the contrast group. These strong relationships support the use of the performance-grouping variable as a holistic and key measure of entrepreneurial performance for evaluating the criterion-related validity of the BP10.

Table 7: Performance Composite Score

	Number of Items	a	Mean	SD	SEM
Performance composite score	9	0.83	-0.015	0.644	0.265

Note:
a = Cronbach's alpha
SD = standard deviation
SEM = standard error of measurement

Concurrent Criterion-Related Validity Coefficients

Table 8 shows the *observed* correlation between the BP10 and the composite performance variable in the fold-back sample. The observed correlation of talents to entrepreneurial success is of similar magnitude as meta-analytic observed correlations reported in Rauch and Frese (2007), where r was 0.231.

Table 8: Relationship Between the BP10 Index Score and Performance

		95% Confidence Interval	
	r^*	Lower Bound	Upper Bound
BP10 Index (n = 905)	0.26	0.19	0.32

* Correlation between BP10 index score and composite performance score is significant at 0.01 level (two-tailed)

Table 9 shows the observed correlations between the talents and the composite performance variable.

Table 9: Relationship Between Theme Scores and Performance

| Talent Themes (n = 905) | r* | 95% Confidence Interval | |
		Lower Bound	Upper Bound
Confidence	0.161	0.09	0.22
Risk	0.241	0.17	0.30
Disruptor	0.116	0.05	0.18
Selling	0.137	0.07	0.20
Profitability	0.199	0.13	0.26
Knowledge	0.130	0.06	0.19
Independence	0.172	0.10	0.23
Determination	0.203	0.13	0.26
Delegator	0.103	0.03	0.16
Relationship	0.164	0.09	0.22

* Correlation between theme score and composite performance score is significant at 0.01 level (two-tailed)

Regression Analysis: Relationship Between Talent and Business Performance

Next, the researchers conducted hierarchical regression analysis to understand the unique contribution of talent in explaining entrepreneurial performance, beyond the size of the company (measured as a dichotomous variable <10 employees = 0, 10+ employees = 1), previous entrepreneurial experience (measured by the number of businesses started), and standard demographic variables such as age and gender.

Table 10 summarizes the results from the hierarchical regression analysis. This approach is appropriate to test whether each new variable or block of variables adds to the prediction produced by the previously entered variables.

The first block of predictors entered in the regression model consisted of age and gender, while the entrepreneurial experience was entered in the second block. The size of the company was entered in the third block, and finally, the Total Index Score was entered in the fourth block. The analysis indicates that each block of variables adds substantially to the explanatory power of the model. Age significantly predicts performance (B = -0.009, t(894) = -4.718, p<0.01), but gender is not significantly related to entrepreneurial performance (B = 0.059, t(894) = 1.348, p = 0.178). However, together they explain 2.8% of the variance in entrepreneurial performance (r = 0.028, p<0.01). The addition of entrepreneurial experience in Model 2 raises the percentage of explained variance from 2.8% to 4.2% (r = 0.042, p<0.01). Experience significantly predicts performance (B = 0.070, t(893) = 3.626, p<0.01). In Model 3, size significantly raises explained variance from 4.2% to 7.1% (r = 0.071, p<0.01) and is a significant predictor of performance (B = 0.405, t(892) = 5.261, p<0.01). In Model 4, talent further raises explained variance from 7.1% to 12.2% (r = 0.122, p<0.01) and is a significant predictor of performance (B = 0.016, t(891) = 7.160, p<0.01).

Table 10: Regression Analysis

	B	Std. Error	Beta	t	Sig.
(Constant)	0.467	0.113		4.144	0.00
Age	-0.009	0.002	-0.157	-4.718	0.00
Gender	0.059	0.043	0.045	1.348	0.17
Experience	0.070	0.019	0.121	3.626	0.00
Size	0.405	0.077	0.173	5.261	0.00
Talent	0.016	0.002	0.235	7.160	0.00

Overall, talent explains about 5% of the variance in entrepreneurial performance after controlling for age, gender, size of the company and previous entrepreneurial experience. This shows that the relationship between talent and performance is substantial.

To understand the practical meaning of the effects detected here, researchers conducted utility analysis. Business impact analysis, or utility analysis, is a means of demonstrating the practical value of the talent-performance linkage in terms of critical business outcomes (Schmidt & Rauschenberger, 1986; Juszkiewicz & Harter, 2003). Table 11 indicates that 32% of those with high talent (based on reference scores; see explanation below) have an average expectation of very high profitability in the next five years, compared with only 6% of those with low talent. Similarly, 40% of high potentials indicate increased hiring, compared with only 23% of low potentials. And 30% of high potentials expect to create jobs in the next five years, compared with only 12% of those with low talent.

Table 11: Utility of Talent

Talent Level	Percentage Who Expect Profit to Be Very High in the Next Five Years	Percentage Who Have Increased the Number of Employees Since the Start of the Business	Percentage Who Expect to Create 5% or More Additional Jobs in the Next Five Years
High potential	32%	40%	30%
Conditional	21%	30%	27%
Low potential	6%	23%	12%

Convergence With Previously Validated Assessments

In developing web-based assessments, Gallup has also studied the convergence of this mode of assessment to traditional structured interviews. In a recent study, Gallup found a high degree of convergence between the two methodologies, with a weighted convergent validity coefficient of 0.62 (Harter & Yang, 2003). Convergence between the web mode and the structured interview is important given that Gallup's structured interviews have a longstanding history of predictive validity across various criterion types (Schmidt & Rader, 1999; Harter, Hayes & Schmidt, 2004). The high level of convergent validity, coupled with predictive and concurrent criterion-related validity evidence, provides considerable evidence to justify the use of the web mode of entrepreneurial talent assessment.

Reference Scores

After researchers finalized the BP10, they set reference scores to differentiate those who have a higher likelihood of success in the entrepreneurial role from others who may need supporting strategies to create or grow sustainable businesses. *Success* in the entrepreneurial role is defined as the creation of a sustainable business with high growth potential.

Researchers derived reference scores based on analysis with the concurrent validation sample and evaluated the scores in terms of their relationships with a job performance measure. That is, researchers set reference scores so that those recommended have a higher probability of success than those not recommended.

Table 12 shows the resulting reference scores, the corresponding classifications and average performance scores.

190

Table 12: Average Performance by Reference Scores

Classification	Reference Scores	Average Performance Score
High potential	75 and above	0.34
Conditional	65-74	0.17
Low potential	0-64	-0.09

High Potential: The individual consistently exhibits behaviors that will allow them to meet most of the demands of the role effectively. They exhibit behaviors that show unique abilities and natural talents for the role.

Conditional: The individual will be able to meet a reasonable number of demands at a high level. However, more deliberate attention to the requirements of the demands is needed to predict consistent success in the role.

Low Potential: Being in the role of an entrepreneur will present challenges for this individual. The actions required to meet the demands might not come naturally to them and often require extra effort and support from others.

Analysis of Adverse Impact Concerning Demographic Variables

Sound instrument development methodology and ongoing validation studies provide the foundation for addressing issues pertaining to the fairness, bias and potential adverse impact concerning using Gallup talent-based selection assessments. Specifically:

- Instrument development research based on a sound methodology provides evidence on the relevance of the content of an assessment to the targeted roles, the psychometric properties of assessment outcomes and concurrent criterion-related validity.

- Ongoing validation studies provide evidence regarding predictive validity and utility of the assessment outcomes, as well as further evidence about these outcomes' psychometric properties.

Additionally, Gallup assesses fairness, bias and potential adverse impact issues in both concurrent instrument development studies and in ongoing validation research.

Researchers can assess bias with various methods, from observing and testing differences in bivariate correlations to sophisticated statistical modeling. In this study, Gallup researchers first compared score distributions among the demographic groups. Table 13 shows these score distributions. Note that researchers did not break out the analysis for race by specific nonwhite race groups because of small sample sizes.[1] Using all cases with valid Theme Index Scores, the effect sizes (standardized mean differences, as measured by Cohen's d_s) were 0.16 for race (with all nonwhite group scoring higher than white), -0.22 for gender (with men scoring higher) and 0.09 for age (with those aged 40 and older scoring higher). These effect sizes may be considered practically small (Cohen, 1988).

Table 13: BP10 Index Score by Demographic Categories

Demographic Group	n	Mean	SD	d_s
Race				
White (not Hispanic or Latino)	825	57.88	9.57	
All nonwhite	70	59.41	10.07	0.16
Gender				
Male	539	58.88	9.81	
Female	366	56.77	9.11	-0.22
Age				
Younger than 40	92	57.35	8.38	
40 and older	759	58.21	9.74	0.09

Analysis of Potential Disparate Impact

Initial estimates of potential disparate impact across demographic groups may be made based on the existing reference scores and using the research sample. Table 14 shows the estimated passing rates (percentage of individuals scored in the "conditional recommend" or the "recommend" range) by demographic group, as well as the associated impact ratio (the ratio of the passing rate of a protected group to the passing rate of an unprotected group). Gallup did not report results for detailed nonwhite groups because of small sample sizes. Numerically, the impact ratio estimates for race and age categories were greater than 0.80, but 0.73 for gender. Furthermore, the 95% confidence intervals of the estimated impact ratios for race and age groups were also above 0.80. This indicates a high degree of

---

1 Gallup's reporting standards require a minimum of 100 cases for reporting passing rates and impact ratios associated with a demographic group. The current sample included 13 Black, 22 American Indian or Alaskan Native, seven Asian (not Hispanic or Latino), three Pacific Islander (not Hispanic or Latino), and 25 Two or More Races.

confidence that the impact ratio would be within the requirement of the four-fifth rule for race and age groups. In summary, these results showed no indication of any substantial disparate impact across race and age groups. However, researchers will continue to monitor adverse impact for gender groups.

Table 14: Estimated Passing Rates and Impact Ratio by Demographics

Demographic Group	Total	Estimated Passing Rate	Estimated Impact Ratio	95% Confidence Interval of Impact Ratio	
				Lower Bound	Upper Bound
Race					
White (not Hispanic or Latino)	825	25.0%			
All nonwhite	70	37.1%	1.49	1.12	1.95
Gender					
Male	539	29.1%			
Female	366	21.3%	0.73	0.60	0.89
Age					
Younger than 40	92	21.7%			
40 and older	759	26.7%	1.23	0.87	1.72

Caveats to the Bias and Adverse Impact Analyses

Together, the results from the analyses of score distributions and of estimated disparate impact suggest that there is no evidence of adverse impact for race and age groups from using the BP10 and the reference scores. However, these analyses are bound by the nature and size of the available data.

First, analyses reported in this paper used participants from the instrument development study. These samples may not represent other entrepreneurs in terms of potential performance in the role, demographics and BP10 Index Score distribution. Thus, researchers will conduct ongoing adverse impact analysis with other participants who take the assessment.

PART II: COLLECTING FURTHER VALIDITY EVIDENCE

Gallup researchers developed the BP10 assessment based on what was learned from the company's long history of developing selection instruments. Part I highlighted instrument development and assessment validation. Part II explains Gallup's continuing efforts to validate the BP10 assessment using diverse samples. The validity evidence outlined in this part further supports the assessment's use.

Researchers know that talent predicts performance in the entrepreneurial role through the empirical studies showing positive correlations across three samples that go beyond the pilot sample. These correlational data are sufficient to show the pervasive predictive validity of entrepreneurial talent to business performance.

The observed correlation of talent to entrepreneurial success is of similar magnitude as meta-analytic observed correlations reported in Rauch and Frese (2007), where r was 0.231. The observed correlations between the predictor (BP10 score) and the criterion variable (the performance metric) in Table 15 are underestimates of the true relationship between entrepreneurial talent and performance. If corrected for criterion variable reliability or range restriction, it is likely to be higher than estimates.

Table 15: Validity of Talent Predicting Business Performance

	Sample Size	Criterion-Related Validity	Version of BP10 Assessment
Pilot sample	905 U.S. entrepreneurs	0.26	Version 1: pilot assessment with 113 items (89 scored)
U.S. high school students	3,119 high school students	0.21	Version 2: high school version with 121 items (93 scored)
Nationally representative sample of entrepreneurs in U.S.	2,697 entrepreneurs	0.25	Version 3: final assessment with 133 items (122 scored)
Mexico City high school students	7,203 high school students	0.20	Version 3: final assessment with 133 items (122 scored)
Inc. 500 sample	155 entrepreneurs	0.18	Version 3: final assessment with 133 items (122 scored)

The BP10 is grounded in cross-cultural research through early qualitative research based on a sample of German entrepreneurs and subsequent samples in Mexico and the U.S. Moreover, the validity coefficients in Table 15 show that the correlations between entrepreneurial talent and business outcomes do not vary substantially across these studies. It appears that the conclusions researchers reached from U.S. samples are not specific to American culture, but they are generalizable across other cultures. Gallup will continue to study cross-cultural issues by conducting comprehensive meta-analysis when gathering data from different countries. The following sections explain each study in Table 15 in detail.

U.S. High School Sample

In May 2013, Gallup researchers tested the BP10 instrument in nine high schools and two entrepreneurship-focus programs for high school students across the state of Nebraska to validate the assessment in a student population. A comprehensive review of the items led to revisions of the assessment. Some of the changes involved removing items that seemed unnecessary and irrelevant to the student population. Based on a review of positive youth development literature, researchers added new items that were more suitable to students' experiential level and stage of life. For instance, researchers replaced items related to delegation and managerial experience with items focused on team participation. The revised instrument consisted of 121 items, of which 93 were scored. There are 82 items common between Version 1 (pilot) and Version 2 (high school) of the assessment.

Findings

Table 16 shows the high school sample broken out by race, gender and grade. All students completed the assessment in U.S. English.

Table 16: Demographics From High School Sample

Variable	In Sample
Total students	3,119
Race	
White (not Hispanic or Latino)	2,098
All nonwhite (not Hispanic or Latino)	679
Black (not Hispanic or Latino)	261
Hispanic or Latino	0
Native American (not Hispanic or Latino)	30
Asian (not Hispanic or Latino)	89
Pacific Islander (not Hispanic or Latino)	18
Other	281
Missing race information	342
Gender	
Male	1,878
Female	1,183
Missing gender information	58
Grade	
9th	1,080
10th	771
11th	775
12th	451
Missing grade information	42

The key criterion measure used in the analysis was a composite of three questions that capture the student's intent to start a business and their formulation of a business idea and a business plan. All items are on a Yes/No scale.

QO1. Are you planning to start your own business in the near future?

QO2. Do you have a business idea you want to try out?

QO3. Do you have a business plan?

Studies indicate that intent is a powerful driver of action (Hurst & Pugsley, 2011); therefore, students with an intent to start a business in the near future are more likely to start a venture than those who do not have an intent to do so. However, just having intent is not a sufficient condition to start a business. An individual's desire to start a venture, if backed by some action, is even more predictive of success. Gallup researchers used "business idea" and "business plan" as proxy for action that would increase the likelihood of starting a business. The composite was formed with unit-weighted z scores of the three measures and is a more holistic and stable measure of entrepreneurial outcomes for evaluating the BP10's criterion-related validity. The validity of talent predicting "plan to start a business" is 0.16, but that increases to 0.21 when combining the three items into a composite performance indicator.

The composite score has values between -0.74 and 1.71.

Table 17: Performance Composite Score for High School Sample

	Number of Items	a	Mean	SD	SEM
Performance composite score	3	0.66	-0.001	0.773	0.450

Note:
a = Cronbach's alpha
SD = standard deviation
SEM = standard error of measurement

Concurrent Criterion-Related Validity Coefficients

Table 18 shows the *observed* correlation between the BP10 and the composite performance variable in the high school sample. The observed correlation of talents to entrepreneurial intent is of similar magnitude as the observed correlations in the fold-back sample, where r was 0.26. This correlation represents the lower-bound estimate of the true relationship between entrepreneurial talent and performance. Once corrected for measurement error and range restriction, the average correlation would be higher than estimated here.

Table 18: Correlation Between BP10 Index Score and Performance for High School Sample

	r^*	95% Confidence Interval	
		Lower Bound	Upper Bound
BP10 Index (n = 3,119)	0.21*	0.17	0.24

* Correlation between BP10 index score and composite performance score is significant at 0.01 level (two-tailed)

Table 19 shows the observed correlations between the talents and the composite performance variable.

Table 19: Relationships Between Theme Scores and Performance for High School Sample

Talent Themes (n = 3,119)	r^*	95% Confidence Interval	
		Lower Bound	Upper Bound
Confidence	0.097	0.062	0.132
Risk	0.294	0.260	0.328
Disruptor	0.207	0.173	0.241
Selling	0.077	0.042	0.112
Profitability	0.045	0.009	0.080
Knowledge	0.101	0.066	0.136
Independence	0.093	0.058	0.128
Determination	0.121	0.086	0.156
Delegator	0.013 (ns)	-0.022	0.048
Relationship	0.116	0.081	0.151

* Correlation between theme score and composite performance score is significant at 0.01 level (two-tailed), except for Delegator

Regression Analysis: Talent Predicts Intent to Start a Business Among High School Students

Next, researchers conducted hierarchical regression analysis to understand the unique contribution of talent in explaining entrepreneurial intent among high school students. Ecological perspective in entrepreneurship research points to the effect of parental business ownership on the likelihood of a child's choice to be an entrepreneur (Sorensen, 2007). Reasons cited include exposure to a business environment through prior work experience in a family member's business (Aldrich & Kim, 2007), acquired knowledge about industry-specific information from parents (Sorensen, 2007), and transfer of social and financial capital from parents to children (Sorensen, 2007). In this analysis, researchers controlled for ecological factors (measured by "Have either of your parents or guardians ever started a business?") to isolate the effect of talent on the likelihood to start a business. In addition, researchers also controlled for standard demographic variables such as race and gender.

Table 20 summarizes the results from the hierarchical regression analysis.

The first block of predictors entered in the regression model consisted of race and gender, while the parental business ownership was entered in the second block. Finally, the Total Index Score was entered in the third block. The analysis indicates that each block of variables adds substantially to the explanatory power of the model. Gender (B = 0.066, t(2769) = 2.203, p<0.01) and race (B = 0.166, t(2769) = 7.605, p<0.01) significantly predict performance. Gender and race explain 2.1% of variance in entrepreneurial outcomes (r = 0.021, p<0.01). The addition of parental business ownership in Model 2 raises the percentage of explained variance from 2.1% to 4.1% (r = 0.041, p<0.01). Ecological factors significantly predict performance (B = 0.229, t(2768) = 7.528, p<0.01). In Model 3, talent further raises explained variance from 4.1% to 7.8% (r = 0.077, p<0.01) and is a significant predictor of performance (B = 0.015, t(2767) = 10.584, p<0.01).

Table 20: Regression Analysis, High School Sample

	B	Std. Error	Beta	t	Sig.
(Constant)	-0.272	0.040		-6.806	0.00
Race	0.166	0.022	0.144	7.605	0.00
Gender	0.066	0.030	0.042	2.203	0.02
Parents own business	0.229	0.030	0.141	7.528	0.00
Talent	0.015	0.001	0.196	10.584	0.00

Overall, talent explains about 4% of the variance in entrepreneurial performance after controlling for race, gender and ecological factors. This shows that the relationship between talent and performance is substantial.

To understand the practical meaning of the effects detected here, researchers conducted utility analysis.

Table 21: Utility of Talent for High School Sample

Talent Level	Percentage Who Expect to Start a Business	Percentage Who Have a Business Idea	Percentage Who Have a Business Plan
High potential	52%	57%	44%
Conditional	40%	52%	31%
Low potential	28%	38%	18%

Table 21 indicates that 52% of those with high talent (based on reference scores) expect to start a business in the near future, compared with 28% of those with low talent. Similarly, 57% of high potentials indicate having a business idea, compared with 38% of low potentials. And 44% of high potentials have a business plan, compared with 18% of those with low talent.

Nationally Representative Sample of Entrepreneurs in the U.S.

Gallup researchers used the findings from the Nebraska high school study to create the final version of the BP10 assessment (Version 3) that reliably measures talent for those aged 14 and older. Version 3 of the assessment consists of 133 items, of which 122 are scored. Version 3 has 53 items in common with Version 1 (pilot assessment) and 58 items in common with Version 2 (high school version). Researchers validated the new assessment using a nationally representative sample of entrepreneurs in the U.S.

Findings

Table 22 shows the national sample broken out by race, gender and age for entrepreneurs and non-entrepreneurs.

Table 22: Demographics From the National Sample of Entrepreneurs

Variable	Entrepreneurs
Total	2,697
Race	
White (not Hispanic or Latino)	2,356
All nonwhite (not Hispanic or Latino)	322
Black (not Hispanic or Latino)	129
Hispanic or Latino	143
Asian (not Hispanic or Latino)	42
Other	8
Missing race information	19
Gender	
Male	1,625
Female	1,072
Missing gender information	0
Age	
Younger than 40	343
40 and older	2,354
Missing age information	0

For the entrepreneur sample, the key criterion measure used in the analysis was a composite of four questions that capture the entrepreneur's intent to grow the business. Researchers formed the composite with unit-weighted z scores of variables:

Q01. In the next 12 months, by what percentage do you expect to increase the number of employees?

Q02. How did your business perform relative to sales goals for the last 12 months?

Q03. How did your business perform relative to profit goals for the last 12 months?

Q04. Thinking ahead to the next five years, which of the following best describes your revenue goals for your business?

The composite score has values between -2.07 and 1.83.

Table 23: Performance Composite Score for the National Sample of Entrepreneurs

	Number of Items	*a*	Mean	SD	SEM
Performance composite score	4	0.54	-0.008	0.687	0.465

Note:
a = Cronbach's alpha
SD = standard deviation
SEM = standard error of measurement

Concurrent Criterion-Related Validity Coefficients

Table 24 shows the *observed* correlation between the BP10 and the composite performance variable in the entrepreneur sample. The observed correlation of talents to entrepreneurial intent is of similar magnitude as the observed correlations in the fold-back sample, where r was 0.26. This correlation represents the lower-bound estimate of the true relationship between entrepreneurial talent and performance. Once corrected for measurement error and range restriction, the average correlation would be higher than estimated here.

Table 24: Relationship Between BP10 Index Score and Performance for National Sample of Entrepreneurs

		95% Confidence Interval	
	r^*	Lower Bound	Upper Bound
BP10 Index (n = 2,697)	0.25*	0.21	0.28

* Correlation between BP10 Index score and composite performance score is significant at 0.01 level (two-tailed)

Table 25 shows the observed correlations between the talents and the composite performance variable.

Table 25: Relationship Between Theme Scores and Performance for National Sample of Entrepreneurs

Talent Themes (n = 2,697)	r^*	95% Confidence Interval	
		Lower Bound	Upper Bound
Confidence	0.168	0.131	0.205
Risk	0.226	0.189	0.263
Disruptor	0.110	0.073	0.148
Selling	0.188	0.151	0.225
Profitability	0.232	0.195	0.268
Knowledge	0.189	0.152	0.226
Independence	0.121	0.084	0.158
Determination	0.182	0.145	0.219
Delegator	0.101	0.063	0.138
Relationship	0.200	0.163	0.237

* Correlation between theme score and composite performance score is significant at 0.01 level (two-tailed)

Regression Analysis: Talent Predicts Performance Among U.S. Sample of Entrepreneurs

Next, researchers conducted hierarchical regression analysis to understand the unique contribution of talent in explaining entrepreneurial performance beyond the size of the company, age of the company and standard demographic variables such as an entrepreneur's age and gender.

The entrepreneur's age is on an interval scale with values ranging from 19 to 66 years and an average entrepreneur age of 48 years. Gender is a dichotomous variable where male = 1 and female = 0. The size of the company is polytomous so that the regression specification requires three dummy variables: one to nine employees, 10 or more employees, and non-employer firms. The non-employer category is the reference group. All respondents who are members of a particular category are assigned a code of 1; respondents not in that particular category receive a code of 0. Finally, the age of the company is measured as a dichotomous variable where zero to five years age = 0; six years and older age = 1.

Table 26 summarizes the results from the hierarchical regression analysis. This approach is appropriate to test whether each new variable or block of variables adds to the prediction produced by the previously entered variables.

The first block of predictors entered in the regression model consisted of the entrepreneur's age and gender, while dummy variables for business age and business size were entered in the second block. Finally, the Total Index Score was entered in the third block.

The analysis indicates that each block of variables adds substantially to the explanatory power of the model. Age (B = -0.012, t(1542) = -8.426, p<0.01) significantly predicts performance. Younger entrepreneurs have higher performance. Gender (B = 0.063, t(1542) = 1.786, p = 0.074) is not a significant predictor, but together they explain about 5% of variance in entrepreneurial outcomes (r = 0.046, p<0.01). The addition of business age and size in Model 2 raises the percentage of explained variance from 5% to 14.3% (r = 0.144, p<0.01). Each factor significantly predicts performance. As expected, younger businesses (zero to five years old) have higher business performance than the more established businesses (B = -0.178, t(1539) = -4.865, p<0.01). Businesses with fewer than 10 employees are performing better than the reference group (non-employers) (B = 0.303, t(1539) = 8.634, p<0.01). Similarly, businesses with 10 or more employees have better business outcomes than the reference group, non-employers (B = 0.720, t(1539) = 12.195, p<0.01). In Model 3, talent further raises explained variance from 14.4% to 18% (r = 0.180, p<0.01) and is a significant predictor of performance (B = 0.013, t(1538) = 8.208, p<0.01).

Table 26: Regression Analysis for National Sample of Entrepreneurs

	B	Std. Error	Beta	t	Sig.
(Constant)	0.581	0.072		7.218	0.00
Age	-0.012	0.001	-0.210	-8.426	0.00
Gender	0.063	0.035	0.044	1.786	0.07
Business age	-0.178	0.037	-0.129	-4.865	0.00
Business size one to nine employees	0.303	0.035	0.219	8.634	0.00
Business size 10+ employees	0.720	0.059	0.310	12.195	0.00
Talent	0.013	0.002	0.195	8.208	0.00

Overall, talent explains about 4% of the variance in entrepreneurial performance after controlling for the entrepreneur's age and gender and the firm's age and size. This shows that the relationship between talent and performance is substantial.

To understand the practical meaning of the effects detected, researchers conducted utility analysis.

Table 27: Utility of Talent for National Sample of Entrepreneurs

Talent Level	Percentage Who Expect to Increase Hiring	Percentage Who Exceeded Sales Goals	Percentage Who Exceeded Profit Goals	Percentage Who Expect to Grow Significantly
High potential	29%	45%	40%	44%
Conditional	21%	22%	19%	35%
Low potential	7%	13%	11%	19%

Table 27 indicates that 29% of those with high talent (based on reference scores) expect to hire in the near future, compared with 7% of those with low talent. Similarly, 45% of high potentials indicate exceeding sales goals, compared with 13% of low potentials. And 40% of high potentials exceeded profit, compared with 11% of those with low talent. Of those with high talent, 44% expect to grow significantly in the next five years, compared with 19% of those with low talent.

Analysis of Adverse Impact With Respect to Demographic Variables

Additionally, Gallup assessed fairness and potential adverse impact issues in the national sample of entrepreneurs as part of the ongoing validation research.

In this study, researchers first compared score distributions among the demographic groups. Table 28 reports these score distributions. Researchers did not break out the analysis for race by specific nonwhite race groups because of small sample sizes[2] for some of the racial groups. Using all cases with valid BP10 scores, the effect sizes (standardized mean differences, as measured by Cohen's d_s) were 0.26 for race (with all nonwhite groups scoring higher than white), -0.34 for gender (with men

---

2 Gallup's reporting standards require a minimum of 100 cases for reporting passing rates and impact ratios associated with a demographic group. In the current sample, there were 129 Black, 42 Asian (not Hispanic or Latino), 143 Hispanic and eight Other.

scoring higher) and -0.07 for age (with those aged younger than 40 scoring higher). These effect sizes may be considered practically small (Cohen, 1988).

Table 28: BP10 Index Score Distributions by Demographics for National Sample of Entrepreneurs

Demographic Group	n	Mean	SD	d_s
Race				
White (not Hispanic or Latino)	2,356	57.45	10.15	
All nonwhite	322	60.09	10.19	0.26
Gender				
Male	1,625	59.39	10.23	
Female	1,072	55.97	9.88	-0.34
Age Group				
Younger than 40	343	58.58	9.51	
40 and older	2,354	57.86	10.47	-0.07

Analysis of Potential Disparate Impact

Researchers made initial estimates of potential disparate impact across demographic groups based on the existing reference scores and using the research sample (see Table 14). Continuing to monitor adverse impact for demographic groups, Table 29 shows the estimated passing rates (percentage of individuals scored in the "conditional recommend" or the "recommend" range) by demographic group, as well as the associated impact ratio (the ratio of the passing rate of a protected group to the passing rate of an unprotected group) for the national sample of entrepreneurs. Gallup did not report results for detailed nonwhite groups because of small sample sizes for some of the minority groups. Numerically, the impact ratio estimates for race and age categories were greater than 0.80, but 0.66 for gender. Furthermore, the 95% confidence intervals of the estimated impact ratios for race and age groups were also above 0.80. This indicates a high degree of confidence that the impact ratio would be within the requirement of the four-fifth rule for race and age groups. In summary, these results showed no indication of any substantial disparate impact across race and age groups. However, researchers will continue to monitor adverse impact for gender groups on an ongoing basis.

Table 29: Estimated Passing Rates and Impact Ratio for U.S. Sample of Entrepreneurs

Demographic Group	Total	Estimated Passing Rate	Estimated Impact Ratio	95% Confidence Interval of Impact Ratio	
				Lower Bound	Upper Bound
Race					
White (not Hispanic or Latino)	2,356	26.7%			
All nonwhite	322	34.5%	1.29	1.13	1.48
Gender					
Male	1,625	31.8%			
Female	1,072	21.1%	0.66	0.59	0.74
Age					
Younger than 40	343	29.4%			
40 and older	2,354	27.3%	0.93	0.80	1.07

Mexico City High School Sample

INADEM, Mexico's federal agency responsible for encouraging and developing entrepreneurial activity in the country, partnered with FONDESO, the state agency for small-business development in Mexico City, to offer an entrepreneurial development program to high school students in Mexico City. The main objective of the program was to identify and develop entrepreneurial talent among high school students in Mexico City. Eight different high school systems participated in the program, which involved talent identification and development of 7,203 students across the city. Researchers used Version 3 (final assessment) to measure talent among these high school students.

Findings

Table 30 shows the national sample broken out by gender for high school students.

Table 30: Demographics of the Mexico City High School Sample

Variable	Entrepreneurs
Total	**7,203**
Gender	
Male	3,250
Female	3,947
Missing gender information	6

For the Mexico City high school student sample, the key criterion measure used in the analysis is the intent to start a business because intent is a strong driver of action. The item "Are you planning to start your own business in the near future?" is on a Yes/No scale. Of the students measured, 81% plan to start a business, which is a relatively high number of students. Social desirability factors could be driving students to say "yes" to the item because they knew that they were invited to be part of a development program sponsored by the federal and state agencies.

Table 31: Performance Metric for the Mexico City High School Sample

Are you planning to start your own business in the near future?	
Yes	81%
No	19%

Concurrent Criterion-Related Validity Coefficients

Table 32 shows the *observed* correlation between the BP10 assessment and the performance variable in the Mexico City sample. The observed correlation of talents to entrepreneurial intent is of similar magnitude as the observed correlations in the fold-back sample, where r was 0.26. This correlation represents the lower-bound estimate of the true relationship between entrepreneurial talent and performance.

Table 32: Relationship Between BP10 Index Score and Performance in Mexico City High School Sample

		95% Confidence Interval	
	r^*	Lower Bound	Upper Bound
BP10 Index (n = 7,203)	0.20*	0.177	0.223

* Correlation between BP10 index score and performance score is significant at 0.01 level (two-tailed)

Table 33 shows the observed correlations between the talents and the performance variable.

Table 33: Relationship Between Theme Scores and Performance in Mexico City High School Sample

Talent (n = 7,203)	r^*	95% Confidence Interval	
		Lower Bound	Upper Bound
Confidence	0.146	0.123	0.168
Risk	0.222	0.199	0.245
Disruptor	0.163	0.140	0.186
Selling	0.093	0.070	0.116
Profitability	0.116	0.093	0.138
Knowledge	0.132	0.109	0.155
Independence	0.127	0.104	0.149
Determination	0.138	0.115	0.161
Delegator	0.036	0.013	0.059
Relationship	0.147	0.124	0.169

* Correlation between theme score and performance score is significant at 0.01 level (two-tailed)

Regression Analysis: Talent Predicts Performance Among Mexico City High School Students

Next, the researchers conducted hierarchical logistic regression to understand the unique contribution of talent in explaining a high school student's intent to start a business, after controlling for gender. Table 34 summarizes the results from the analysis.

In the first block, researchers entered gender. The Total Index Score was entered in the second block. The analysis indicates that each block of variables adds substantially to the explanatory power of the model. Gender (χ^2 = 10.92, df = 1, n = 6,675, p<0.01) significantly predicts performance. Males are more likely to say that they intend to start a business in the near future. Gender explains

0.3% of variance in entrepreneurial outcome (Nagelkerke, r = 0.003). In Model 2, researchers entered talent score to see if it would add to the predictive power of gender. It does, as indicated by the results of block 2 ($\mathcal{X}^2$ = 246.36, df = 1, n = 6,675, p<0.01). Talent substantially raises explained variance from 0.3% to 6% (Nagelkerke, r = 0.061) and is a significant predictor of performance.

Table 34: Regression Analysis for Mexico City High School Sample

	B	Wald $\mathcal{X}^2$	p	Odds Ratio
(Constant)	-1.568	64.363	0.000	0.208
Gender	0.164	6.271	0.012	1.178
Talent	0.056	228.320	0.000	1.058

Overall, talent explains about 6% of the variance in intent to start a business, after controlling for gender. This shows that the relationship between talent and performance is substantial.

To understand the practical meaning of the effects detected here, researchers conducted utility analysis.

Table 35: Utility of Talent for Mexico City High School Sample

Talent Level	Percentage Who Expect to Start a Business
High potential	92%
Conditional	91%
Low potential	79%

Table 35 indicates that 92% of those with high talent expect to start a business in the near future, compared with 79% of those with low talent.

Inc. 500 Sample

This study includes 155 CEOs from the Inc. 500 fastest growing private companies that completed the Gallup BP10 assessment.

Findings

Table 36 shows the Inc. 500 sample by entrepreneurs' race, gender and age.

Table 36: Demographics of the Inc. 500 Sample

Variable	n
Race	
White (not Hispanic or Latino)	112
Black	2
Native Hawaiian or Pacific Islander	1
Asian	17
American Indian or Alaska Native	1
Two or more races	8
Missing race information	14
Gender	
Male	140
Female	13
Missing gender information	2
Age	
Younger than 40	73
40 and older	82

Overall Distribution of Talent

The Inc. 500 entrepreneurs score much higher on the BP10 assessment compared with the national sample of entrepreneurs in Gallup's database. The national sample of entrepreneurs has an average talent score of 58.40, while the Inc. 500 sample has an average score of 72.46.

Table 37: BP10 Score Differences Between Inc. 500 and National Sample of Entrepreneurs

	Mean	N	Standard Deviation
Inc. 500	72.46	155	7.68
National sample of entrepreneurs	58.41	2,697	9.89

Overall Distribution of Talent
Inc. 500 Entrepreneurs vs. National Sample

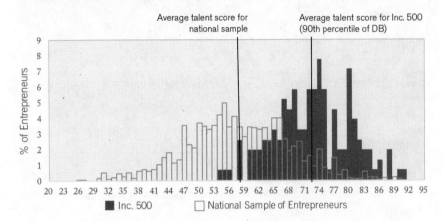

Next, Gallup researchers conducted the independent samples t-test to compare the means of the national sample of entrepreneurs with the Inc. 500 sample to determine whether there is statistical evidence that the associated population means are significantly different.

The results indicate a significant difference in the talent scores for the Inc. 500 (M = 72.46, SD = 7.68) and national sample of entrepreneurs (M = 58.41, SD = 9.89); $t_{184.710}$ = 21.771, p<0.001.

The average talent score for the Inc. 500 sample is 14 points above the average talent score for the national sample of entrepreneurs.

Table 38: Independent Samples T-Test: Comparing National Sample of Entrepreneurs to the Inc. 500 Sample

	Levene's Test for Equality of Variances		T-Test for Equality of Means						
	F	Sig.	t	df	Sig. (2-tailed)	Mean Difference	Std. Error Difference	95% Confidence Interval of the Difference	
								Lower	Upper
Equal variances assumed	12.999	0	-17.381	2850	0	-14.05703	0.80878	-15.6429	-12.47117
Equal variances not assumed			-21.771	184.7	0	-14.05703	0.64569	-15.3309	-12.78315

For the Inc. 500 sample, Gallup researchers used four questions that capture an entrepreneur's intent to grow a business. Researchers created the questions using unit-weighted z scores of variables:

Q01. In the next 12 months, by what percentage do you expect to increase the number of employees?

Q02. How did your business perform relative to sales goals for the last 12 months?

Q03. How did your business perform relative to profit goals for the last 12 months?

Q04. Thinking ahead to the next five years, which of the following best describes your revenue goals for your business?

The composite score has values between -3.34 and 0.64.

Table 39: Performance Composite Score for the Inc. 500 Entrepreneurs

	N	Minimum	Maximum	Mean	Standard Deviation
Performance composite score	147	-3.34	0.64	0.009	0.65150

Concurrent Criterion-Related Validity Coefficients

Table 40 shows the observed correlation between the BP10 and the composite performance variable in the Inc. 500 sample. The observed correlation of talents to entrepreneurial intent is of similar magnitude as the observed correlations in the fold-back sample, where r was 0.26. This correlation represents the lower-bound estimate of the true relationship between entrepreneurial talent and performance. Once corrected for measurement error and range restriction, the average correlation would be higher than estimated here.

Table 40: Relationship Between BP10 Index Score and Performance for Inc. 500 Sample

	Correlation	95% Confidence Interval	
		Lower Bound	Upper Bound
BP10 Index (n = 155)	0.183*	0.021	0.335

* Correlation between BP10 Index score and composite performance score is significant at 0.01 level (two-tailed)

PART III: RECONFIGURING THE BUILDER PROFILE 10

Building on the previous research studies, Gallup researchers reconfigured the BP10 assessment in 2015. The most recent version of the assessment consists of a new item type. The reconfigured BP10 assessment has 111-paired-comparison statements. Each item is a pair of potential self-descriptors. The descriptors are anchored to opposite ends of the scale. During the assessment, respondents choose the statement that best describes them. Participants have up to 20 seconds to respond to a given item before the system moves on to the next item. Developmental research showed that the 20-second limit resulted in a negligible item noncompletion rate.

The figure below shows an example of the BP10 assessment item format that appears on participants' computer screen.

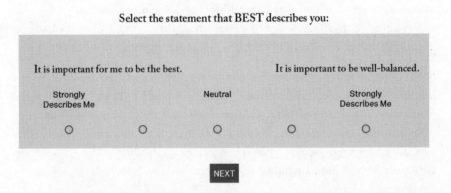

Select the statement that BEST describes you:

It is important for me to be the best.   It is important to be well-balanced.

Strongly   Neutral   Strongly
Describes Me   Describes Me

○   ○   ○   ○   ○

NEXT

Only one of the descriptors in an item is the "correct" answer and is associated with a BP10 "theme." A theme is a category of talents, which Gallup defines as recurring and consistent patterns of thought, feeling or behavior. The BP10 assessment measures the presence of talent in 10 distinct themes. Each response to an item can contribute to only one theme; a descriptor will not connect to more than one theme. Multiple items on the assessment measure a theme. A proprietary formula assigns a value to each response category. Researchers aggregate values for items in the theme to derive a theme score.

Researchers base the calculation of the scores on the mean of the intensity of self-description. Scores are recorded in Gallup's database as theme means and standard scores.

Gallup researchers reconfigured the assessment and changed the item type to reduce acquiescence response bias and social desirability bias and to increase measurement precision.

Acquiescence response bias is the tendency for survey respondents to agree with statements regardless of their content. The previous version of the BP10 assessment had Likert scale and multiple-choice items. Likert items, which have scale end points of "strongly disagree" and "strongly agree," are particularly susceptible to acquiescence response bias. Some respondents might take mental shortcuts when they are responding to questions on a Likert scale. This tendency to answer positively is one of those common shortcuts.

In addition, the social norm of appearing agreeable and polite can bias respondents, even when they are taking the assessment anonymously. This makes them more likely to avoid disagreeing. Presenting paired-comparison items reduces the likelihood of choosing the more agreeable response.

Social desirability bias refers to the fact that in self-reports, people often report inaccurately to present themselves in the best possible light. Though social desirability can affect the validity of experimental and survey research findings, using paired-comparison items is an effective way to prevent or reduce social desirability bias. By generating questions that are equal in desirability in the reconfigured BP10, researchers have attempted to prevent a socially desirable response in one direction or another.

The reconfiguration of the BP10 assessment has also increased measurement precision and accuracy, as evidenced by higher reliability and validity scores.

Psychometric Properties of the Reconfigured BP10 Assessment

The new BP10 assessment has 111-paired-comparison items, of which 93 are scored.

Sample

Researchers validated the new assessment using the sample of 3,804 respondents from the Gallup panel.

Table 41: Sample

	Respondents
Entrepreneurs	1,514
Non-entrepreneurs	2,282
Missing	8
Total sample	**3,804**

Table 42: Demographics

Variable	Total Sample	Entrepreneurs	Non-Entrepreneurs
Race			
White (not Hispanic or Latino)	3,369	1,348	2,013
Black	150	65	85
Asian	54	14	40
Hispanic	191	73	118
Other	10	2	8
Missing race information	30	12	18
Gender			
Male	2,098	921	1,172
Female	1,706	593	1,110
Age			
Younger than 40	483	145	338
40 and older	3,321	1,369	1,944

Reliability of the Index Score

Table 43 shows the internal consistency reliability of the reconfigured BP10 assessment.

Table 43: Reliability and Descriptive Statistics for the BP10 Assessment

Index	Number of Items	a	Mean	SD	SEM
BP10	93	0.88	49.65	8.74	3.03

Note:
a = Cronbach's alpha
SD = standard deviation
SEM = standard error of measurement

Table 44: Reliability and Descriptive Statistics for Talent Theme Scores

	Number of Items	a	Mean	SD
Profitability	8	0.643	36.25	15.15
Confidence	8	0.587	43.79	14.91
Disruptor	9	0.583	52.91	14.47
Delegator	7	0.335	52.91	14.33
Determination	11	0.768	59.54	16.41
Independence	10	0.692	52.24	15.91
Knowledge	7	0.344	55.21	13.87
Selling	12	0.696	42.35	14.92
Relationship	10	0.695	47.82	16.33
Risk	11	0.576	53.35	13.19

Note:
a = Cronbach's alpha
SD = standard deviation

Comparing Entrepreneurs With Non-Entrepreneurs

The BP10 assessment differentiates between entrepreneurs and non-entrepreneurs. As expected, entrepreneurs score significantly higher on the assessment compared with non-entrepreneurs.

Table 45: Average Talent Score for Entrepreneurs and Non-Entrepreneurs

	Mean	N	Standard Deviation
Entrepreneurs	52.23	1,514	8.74
Non-entrepreneurs	47.94	2,282	8.30

The researchers conducted the independent samples t-test to compare the means of entrepreneurs and non-entrepreneurs to determine whether there is statistical evidence that the associated population means are significantly different.

The results indicate that there is a significant difference in the talent scores for entrepreneurs (M = 52.23, SD = 8.74) and non-entrepreneurs (M = 47.94, SD = 8.30); $t_{3,122.94}$ = 15.135, p<0.001.

The average talent score for the entrepreneurs is four points above the average talent score for the non-entrepreneurs.

Table 46: Independent Samples Test

		Levene's Test for Equality of Variances		T-Test for Equality of Means					95% Confidence Interval of the Difference	
		F	Sig.	t	df	Sig. (2-tailed)	Mean Difference	Std. Error Difference	Lower	Upper
Percentage score of 93 final items	Equal variances assumed	5.798	0.016	15.294	3,794	0.000	4.29604	0.28089	3.74533	4.84676
	Equal variances not assumed			15.135	3,122.943	0.000	4.29604	0.28386	3.73948	4.85261

Concurrent Criterion–Related Validity Coefficients

Table 47 shows the observed correlation between the new BP10 assessment and the composite performance variable. The composite performance variable is the composite of the same four questions used in the previous version of the BP10 assessment.

Researchers did not correct the observed correlation to performance for measurement error in the criterion measure, so it is likely to be an underestimate of the relationship between the total score and entrepreneurial performance. Past research has shown that composite performance measures have a reliability of 0.75 (Harter, Hayes & Schmidt, 2004). The researchers corrected the criterion-related validity coefficient for composite reliability.

Given two random variables X and Y, with correlation rxy, and a composite reliability of the performance measure r_{yy} (r_{yy} = 0.75), the correlation between X and Y corrected for attenuation is:

$$R_{x'y'} = \frac{r_{xy}}{\sqrt{r_{yy}}}$$

Table 47: Relationship Between the BP10 Index Score and Performance

	Uncorrected Coefficient	95% Confidence Interval		Corrected Criterion Validity (Reliability = 0.75)
		Lower Bound	Upper Bound	
BP10 Index	0.279	0.227	0.329	0.322

Table 48 shows the observed correlations between the talent themes and the composite performance.

Table 48: Correlation Between Talent Theme and Composite Performance

	Correlation	95% Confidence Interval	
		Lower Bound	Upper Bound
Profitability	0.153	0.099	0.207
Confidence	0.201	0.147	0.254
Disruptor	0.115	0.060	0.169
Delegator	0.111	0.056	0.165
Determination	0.167	0.113	0.221
Independence	0.173	0.119	0.227
Knowledge	0.156	0.101	0.209
Selling	0.169	0.115	0.223
Relationship	0.130	0.075	0.184
Risk	0.237	0.184	0.288

Missing value handling: PAIRWISE, EXCLUDE. C.I. Level: 95.0

Interpreting Criterion Validity Coefficients

Criterion-related validity evidence is typically expressed as correlations. But are these correlations meaningful? Such a question needs to be answered within the relevant context. The first context is the findings in the literature regarding the criterion-related validity of other personality assessments. Published meta-analytical studies regarding the predictability of dispositional factors to entrepreneurship effectiveness show a correlation of 0.24 with business success (Frese and Gielnik, 2014). Other studies have reported true score correlations between personality characteristics and entrepreneurial outcomes ranging from 0.10 to 0.38. The relationship varies depending on the type of outcome measure used. For instance, self-efficacy shows a relationship to business creation, $r = 0.28$ (Rauch & Frese, 2007), while innovativeness is related to business creation ($r = 0.24$) and business performance ($r = 0.27$) (Rauch & Frese, 2007). On the other hand, risk propensity has a correlation of 0.10 to both business creation and business performance (Rauch & Frese, 2007). The estimated criterion validity with the Gallup BP10 total score appears to be comparable to those reported by Rauch and Frese (2007).

Another context for understanding the magnitude of a validity coefficient is to consider its practical business impact or potential utility. There are established methods to estimate impact from implementing a selection/identification approach. Theoretical expectancy models (Taylor & Russell, 1939) show that, holding validity constant, the practical gain from a selection/identification procedure may increase as a result of decreasing selection ratio and may also be affected by the base rate of success in the role (i.e., the rate of success without using the selection/identification tool). For example, assuming a 19% base rate of success among entrepreneurs (19% of entrepreneurs in the probability-based sample have a company with revenue of $1 million or more) and applying the 0.279 validity coefficient, selecting the top 5% of respondents (those with high talent) would improve the rate of success to 40%, or an improvement of 110%. In odds ratio terms, this means that it is more than two times as likely to find a successful entrepreneur ("successful" as defined by those with revenue over $1 million) by using the assessment compared with random selection (leaving it to chance).

These types of utility estimates can be calculated for many of the outcomes entrepreneurs are responsible for. In short, if the Gallup BP10 assessment is used systematically in early identification and development of talent, our economies can expect to see sizable practical gains over time.

Convergent Validity

In developing the reconfigured assessment, Gallup studied the convergence of the new assessment to the previous version of BP10. Of the 3,804 who completed the reconfigured assessment, 3,254 have also completed the previous version of BP10.

Researchers found a high degree of convergence between the two assessments, with a convergent validity of 0.73. The high level of convergent validity coupled with concurrent criterion-related validity evidence provides considerable evidence to justify the use of the reconfigured BP10.

Further, the researchers corrected the convergent validity coefficient for reliabilities. Correlations between parameters are diluted or weakened by measurement error. Disattenuation provides for a more accurate estimate of the correlation between the parameters by accounting for this effect.

Expressed in terms of classical test theory, the convergent validity coefficient is divided by the geometric mean of the reliability coefficients of two assessments. Given two random variables X and Y, with correlation r_{xy}, and a known reliability for each variable, r_{xx} and r_{yy}, the correlation between X and Y corrected for attenuation is:

$$R_{x'y'} = \frac{r_{xy}}{\sqrt{r_{xx} \cdot r_{yy}}}$$

Table 49: Corrected Convergent Validity

	Convergent Validity	Cronbach's Alpha for New BP10	Cronbach's Alpha for BP10 Version 3	Corrected Convergent Validity
Overall talent score	0.732	0.883	0.937	0.805

Table 50: Theme-Level Convergent Validity

BP10 Theme	Convergent Validity
Profitability	0.447
Confidence	0.368
Disruptor	0.579
Delegator	0.322
Determination	0.645
Independence	0.620
Knowledge	0.433
Selling	0.470
Relationship	0.632
Risk	0.490

Conclusion

The evidence presented in this part supports the hypothesis that entrepreneurial talent relates positively to business outcomes such as higher profitability, increased hiring and higher revenue. The studies outlined in this part also show that those with higher levels of entrepreneurial talent are more likely to say that they intend to grow their business. The preponderance of the validity evidence to date shows strong evidence of the utility of BP10 in driving business outcomes. Gallup continues to study the relationships between talent and business performance as data become available from clients and research partners.

PART IV: ASSESSMENT DETAILS

Administration

Before implementing the BP10, users should address issues pertaining to the proper administration of the assessment such as reporting structure, software/hardware availability and accessibility, security, and confidentiality. Focus discussions of these issues on providing a fair and secure assessment environment for all participants. In addition, focus discussions on establishing systems that allow for accurate and efficient delivery and access of assessment outcomes. Finally, Gallup must train and certify BP10 assessment users as part of the assurance of proper interpretation and use of the assessment.

Feedback

After completing the BP10 assessment, individuals receive a customized report based on their scores in each of the 10 talents. Individuals do not see their scores because the talents appear in order of intensity. In programs designed to develop entrepreneurial talent, the customized report becomes the basis for coaching and mentoring by Gallup-trained coaches. Gallup designed the report to help individuals develop their entrepreneurial talents and manage areas of lesser talents.

The number of possible permutations of rank-ordered talents is large. There are 3,628,800 possible permutations (order-dependent), making it rare for two individuals to have the same rank order of talents. Taking into consideration talent intensity and rank order, the number of possible permutations exceeds 214 billion. This means that the probability of finding two individuals with the same rank order *and* same intensity of talents is effectively zero.

Proper Use of Assessment Outcomes

Applications of the BP10 are consistent with the instrument development process, which relevant validity evidence supports. Gallup will not support or defend improper uses of the assessment.

Although the assessment includes items about a range of interrelated topics, Gallup created these items for facilitating decisions about entrepreneurial potential at the Index Total Score level only. The Talent-Based Index is designed so that higher-scoring individuals are potentially more likely to be successful in the entrepreneurial role than lower-scoring individuals. However, Gallup recommends using the assessment results to help individuals understand how they can best use their talents to drive business success. The issue is not so much of "how much more" talent one individual has over another, but how each individual can realize and best put their talents to use in the role. The assessment results should not be used to determine who should be an entrepreneur because compensatory actions — such as the formation of complementary partnerships, acquiring skills or knowledge, or putting systems in place to manage areas of less talent — can lead to business success.

Individuals also receive a report with the 10 talents arranged in descending order based on the intensity score as part of the assessment outcomes. The theme report provides detailed information about an individual's talent profile. The talent themes and the BP10 Index Total Score are the best representation of a person's talents and can be used to devise proper strategies to help individuals maximize their talents. Proper use and interpretation of Total Index Scores and talent reports require training from an experienced Gallup consultant. Gallup will not support or defend improper uses of these reports.

Studies indicate that the interaction between specific traits and environmental factors predicts business success better than any one of these factors alone (Bandura, 1986; Barrick, Mitchell & Steward, 2003; Hattrup & Jackson, 1996). Hence, consider factors such as market conditions, role of government, social environment, access to information, access to credit, infrastructure and other relevant information when making informed judgments about an entrepreneur's potential.

REFERENCES

Ackerman, P.L., & Cianciolo, A.T. (2000). Cognitive, perceptual-speed, and psychomotor determinants of individual differences during skill acquisition. *Journal of Experimental Psychology: Applied*, *6*(4), 259-290.

Acs, Z.J., Desai, S., & Hessels, J. (2008). Entrepreneurship, economic development and institutions. *Small Business Economics: An Entrepreneurship Journal*. Retrieved from http://link.springer.com/article/10.1007/s11187-008-9135-9/fulltext.html

Aldrich, H.E., Carter, N.M., and Ruef, M. (2004). "Teams." In W.B. Gartner, K.G. Shaver, N.M. Carter, and P. Reynolds (Eds.), *Handbook of Entrepreneurial Dynamics: The Process of Business Creation*. Thousand Oaks, CA: Sage, pp. 299-310.

Aldrich, H.E., & Kim, P.H. (2007). Small worlds, infinite possibilities? How social networks affect entrepreneurial team formation and search. *Strategic Entrepreneurship Journal*, *1*(1-2), 147-165.

American Educational Research Association, American Psychological Association, and National Council on Measurement in Education. (1999). *Standards for Educational and Psychological Testing*. Washington, D.C.: American Educational Research Association.

Arenius, P., & Minniti, M. (2005). Perceptual variables and nascent entrepreneurship. *Small Business Economics*, *24*, 233-247.

Arora, A., Cohen, W.M., and Walsh, J.P. (2016). The acquisition and commercialization of invention in American manufacturing: Incidence and impact. *Research Policy*, *45*(6), 1113-1128.

Badal, S.B. (2010). *Entrepreneurship and job creation: Leveraging the relationship*. Gallup White Paper: Omaha, NE.

Baker, T., Miner, A., & Eesley, D. (2003). Improvising firms: Bricolage, account giving and improvisational competencies in the founding process. *Research Policy*, *32*(2). 255-276.

Bandura, A. (1986). *Social foundations of thought and action*. Englewood Cliffs, NJ: Prentice Hall.

Baron, R.A. (2006). Opportunity recognition as pattern recognition: How entrepreneurs "connect the dots" to identify new business opportunities. *Academy of Management Perspectives*, *20*(1), 104-119.

Barrick, M.R., Mitchell, T.R., & Steward, G.L. (2003). Situational and motivational influences on trait-behavior relationships. In M.R. Barrick & A.M. Ryan (Eds.), *Personality and work: Reconsidering the role of personality on organizations*, 60-82. San Francisco, CA: Jossey-Bass.

Barrick, M.R., & Mount, M.K. (1991). The big five personality dimensions and job performance: A meta-analysis. *Personnel Psychology*, *41*(1), 1-26.

Baum, J.R., Frese, M., & Baron, R.A. (2006). *The psychology of entrepreneurship*. New York: Psychology Press.

Berman, E. (2017, April 24). American Voices: John Leguizamo, actor. *Time*. Retrieved November 8, 2017, from http://time.com/collection/american-voices-2017/4738017/john-leguizamo-american-voices/

Birley, S., and Stockley, S. (2000). "Entrepreneurial teams and venture growth." In H. Landstrom (Ed.), *The Blackwell handbook of entrepreneurship*. Hoboken, NJ: Wiley-Blackwell. pp. 287-307.

Bögenhold, D. (1987). *De gründerboom: Realität und mythos der neuen selbständigkeit*, Campus Verlag GmbH: Frankfurt, Germany.

Brandstatter, H. (1997). Becoming an entrepreneur — a question of personality structure? *Journal of Economic Psychology, 18*, 157-177.

Breedlove, S. (2017). *All in: How women entrepreneurs can think bigger, build sustainable businesses, and change the world*. Austin, TX: Greenleaf Book Group Press.

Brown, J. (2013, March 10). *20 unstoppable entrepreneurs share their advice for success*. Retrieved December 1, 2017, from http://addicted2success.com/success-advice/20-unstoppable-entrepreneurs-share-their-advice-for-success/

Bygrave, W.D. (1989). The entrepreneurship paradigm: A philosophical look at its research methodologies. *Entrepreneurship Theory and Practice, Fall*, 7-26.

Campbell, A. (2013, September 5). *6 rules of entrepreneurship from founders in the trenches*. Retrieved December 1, 2017, from http://www.innovationamerica.us/index.php/innovation-daily/32355-rules-of-entrepreneurship-from-founders-in-the-trenches?utm_source=innovation-daily---your-daily-newsletter-highlighting-global-innovation-news-and-trends&utm_medium=gazetty&utm_campaign=09-09-2013

Campos, et al. (2017). Teaching personal initiative beats traditional training in boosting small business in West Africa. *Science, 357*(6357), 1287-1290.

Chell, E., Haworth, J.M., & Brearley, S. (1991). *The entrepreneurial personality: Concepts, cases, and categories*. Hampshire, United Kingdom: Cengage Learning EMA.

Chen, C.C., Greene, P.G., & Crick, A. (1998). Does entrepreneurial self-efficacy distinguish entrepreneurs from managers? *Journal of Business Venturing, 13*, 295-316.

Ciaverella, M.A., Bucholtz, A.K, Riordan, C.M., Gatewood, R.D., & Stokes, G.S. (2004). The big five and venture success: Is there a linkage? *Journal of Business Venturing, 19*(4), 465-483.

Clifton, D.O., & Nelson, P. (1992). *Soar with your strengths*. New York: Delacorte Press.

Cohen, J. (1988). *Statistical power analysis for the behavioral sciences (2nd ed.)*. Hillsdale, NJ: Lawrence Erlbaum Associates.

Collins, C.J., Hanges, P.J., & Locke, E.A. (2004). The relationship of achievement motivation to entrepreneurial behavior: A meta-analysis. *Human Performance, 17*, 95-117.

Company history. (n.d.). Retrieved November 20, 2017, from https://aboutschwab.com/about/history

Content Marketing Institute. (2012, September 27). *What is content marketing?* Retrieved November 15, 2017, from http://contentmarketinginstitute.com/what-is-content-marketing/

Csikszentmihalyi, M. (1996). *Creativity: Flow and the psychology of discovery and invention.* New York, NY: Harper Perennial.

Csikszentmihalyi, M. (2016, September 10). *The pursuit of happiness.* Retrieved November 15, 2017, from http://www.pursuit-of-happiness.org/history-of-happiness/mihaly-csikszentmihalyi/

Davidsson, P., & Honig, B. (2003). The role of social and human capital among nascent entrepreneurs. *Journal of Business Venturing, 18*, 301-331.

Dell, M., & Fredman, C. (1999). *Direct from Dell: Strategies that revolutionized an industry.* New York: HarperBusiness.

Deutschman, A. (2004, August 1). *Inside the mind of Jeff Bezos.* Retrieved December 1, 2017, from http://www.fastcompany.com/50541/inside-mind-jeff-bezos

Deutschman, A. (2004, December 1). *The fabric of creativity.* Retrieved November 8, 2017, from https://www.fastcompany.com/51733/fabric-creativity

Dimov, D.P., & Shepherd, D.A. (2005). Human capital theory and venture capital firms: Exploring "home runs" and "strike outs." *Journal of Business Venturing, 20*, 1-21.

Duchesneau, D.A., & Gartner, W.B. (1990). A profile of new venture success and failure in an emerging industry. *Journal of Business Venturing, 5*, 297-312.

Dyson, J. (2005, September). James Dyson on innovation. *Ingenia, 24*, 31-34.

Engle, D.E., Mah, J.J., & Sadri, G. (1997). An empirical comparison of entrepreneurs and employees: Implications for innovation. *Creativity Research Journal, 10*, 45-49.

Federal Reserve Bank of New York. (2017, October 4). *The labor market for recent college graduates: Underemployment.* Retrieved November 8, 2017, from https://www.newyorkfed.org/research/college-labor-market/college-labor-market_underemployment_rates.html

Federal Reserve Bank of New York. (2017, October 4). *The labor market for recent college graduates: Unemployment.* Retrieved November 8, 2017, from https://www.newyorkfed. org/research/college-labor-market/college-labor-market_unemployment.html

Frese, M., & Geilnik, M.M. (2014). The psychology of entrepreneurship. *The Annual Review of Organizational Psychology and Organizational Behavior, 1,* 413-438.

Gladwell, M. (2009, July 27). *Cocksure: Banks, battles, and the psychology of overconfidence.* Retrieved November 6, 2017, from http://www.newyorker.com/ reporting/2009/07/27/090727fa_fact_gladwell?currentPage=all

Guber, P. (2011). *Tell to win: Connect, persuade, and triumph with the hidden power of story.* New York: Crown Business.

Haber, S., & Reichel, A. (2007). The cumulative nature of the entrepreneurial process: The contribution of human capital, planning and environment resources to small venture performance. *Journal of Business Venturing, 22,* 119-145.

Hansen, K. (2011). Booyah: When a business makes its first million dollars in revenue. *CNN Money.* Retrieved December 13, 2017, from http://money.cnn.com/2011/07/11/ smallbusiness/first_million_dollars/index.htm

Harley-Davidson Motor Company. (2012, September 10). *Harley-Davidson calls on fans to unleash their own personal freedom and independence.* Retrieved December 1, 2017, from http://investor.harley-davidson.com/mobile.view?c=87981&v=203&d=1&id=1733717

Harrington, A. (2003, November 10). Who's afraid of a new product? Not W.L. Gore. It has mastered the art of storming completely different businesses. *Fortune magazine.* Retrieved November 8, 2017, from http://archive.fortune.com/magazines/fortune/ fortune_archive/2003/11/10/352851/index.htm

Harter, J.K. (2003). *Test-retest reliability of Gallup SRI assessments.* Gallup Technical Report: Omaha, NE.

Harter, J.K., Hayes, T.L., & Schmidt, F.L. (2004). *Meta-analytic predictive validity of Gallup Selection Research Instruments (SRI).* Gallup Technical Report: Omaha, NE.

Harter, J.K., & Yang, Y. (2003). *Convergent validity of Gallup SRI assessment modes.* Gallup Technical Report: Omaha, NE.

Hattrup, K., & Jackson, S.E. (1996). *Learning about individual differences by taking situations seriously.* San Francisco, CA: Jossey-Bass.

Hite, J.M., & Hesterly, W.S. (March 2001). The evolution of firm networks: From emergence to early growth of the firm. *Strategic Management Journal, 22*(3), 275-286.

Hoelzl, E., & Rustichini, A. (2005). Overconfident: Do you put your money on it? *The Economic Journal, 115,* 305-324.

Hunter, J.E. (1986). Cognitive ability, cognitive aptitudes, job knowledge, and job performance. *Journal of Vocational Behavior, 29*, 340-362.

Hurst, E., & Pugsley, B.W. (2011). *What do small businesses do?* NBER Working Paper No. 17041. National Bureau of Economic Research, Cambridge, MA.

Intrapreneurship. (2010, November 1). *Case study of intrapreneurship success — WL Gore Associates, Inc.* [Web log post]. Retrieved November 8, 2017, from http://rollinsintrapreneur.blogspot.com/2010/11/case-study-of-intrapreneurship-success.html

Judge, T.A., Bono, J.E., & Gerhardt, M.W. (2002). Personality and leadership: A qualitative and quantitative review. *Journal of Applied Psychology, 87*(4), 765-780.

Juszkiewicz, P.J., & Harter, J.K. (2003). *Utility analysis of Gallup SRI assessments.* Gallup Technical Report: Omaha, NE.

Kahn, J. (2012, April 5). *Larry Page posts 'Update from the CEO 2012' memo detailing Google's aspirations.* Retrieved December 1, 2017, from https://9to5google.com/2012/04/05/larry-page-posts-update-from-the-ceo-2012%E2%80%B3-memo-detailing-googles-aspirations/

Kavanagh, J. (2007, May 21). *Roy Spence: Founder and president GSD&M.* Retrieved November 15, 2017, from http://www.sportsbusinessdaily.com/Journal/Issues/2007/05/20070521/One-On-One/Roy-Spence-Founder-And-President-GSDM.aspx

Koellinger P., Minniti, M., & Schade, C. (2007). I think I can, I think I can ... A study of entrepreneurial behavior. *Journal of Economic Psychology, 28*, 502-527.

Kopf, D. (2016, December 5). *Almost all the US jobs created since 2005 are temporary.* Retrieved November 20, 2017, from http://qz.com/851066/almost-all-the-10-million-jobs-created-since-2005-are-temporary/

Kunreuther, H., Meyer, R., Zeckhauser, R., Slovic, P., Schwartz, B., Schade, C., Luce, M.F., Lippman, S., Krantz, D., Kahn, B., & Hogarth, R. (2002). High stakes decision making: Normative, descriptive and prescriptive considerations. *Marketing Letters, 13*, 259-268.

Lerner, M., & Haber, S. (2001). Performance factors of small tourism ventures: The interface of tourism, entrepreneurship and the environment. *Journal of Business Venturing, 16*, 77-100.

Loewenstein, G. (1992). The fall and rise of psychological explanations in the economics of intertemporal choice. In G. Loewenstein & J. Elster (Eds.). *Choice over time.* New York: Russell Sage.

Loomis, C. (2012). *Tap dancing to work: Warren Buffett on practically everything, 1966-2012: A Fortune magazine book.* New York: Portfolio/Penguin.

Lowe, J. (2007). *Warren Buffett speaks: Wit and wisdom from the world's greatest investor.* Hoboken, New Jersey: Wiley.

Luchies, M. (2013, September 4). *Starting a business as a young entrepreneur: Interview with Sachin Kamdar, CEO of Parse.ly.* Retrieved December 1, 2017, from http://under30ceo.com/succeeding-over-obstacles-interview-with-sachin-kamdar-ceo-of-parse-ly/#f1lMfLXbxPBwDwEA.99

Manjoo, F. (2011, August 1). *People will misunderstand you.* Retrieved December 1, 2017, from http://www.slate.com/articles/technology/top_right/2011/08/people_will_misunderstand_you.html

McCloskey, H. (2015, July 14). *The 1-2-3's of A/B testing: An intro to split and multivariate tests for product managers.* Retrieved November 20, 2017, from https://community.uservoice.com/blog/ab-split-testing-product/

Minniti, M., & Nardone, C. (2007). Being in someone else's shoes: Gender and nascent entrepreneurship. *Small Business Economics Journal, 28*(2-3), 223-239.

Morris, M.H., Avila, R.A., & Allen, J. (1993). Individualism and the modern corporation: Implications for innovation and entrepreneurship. *Journal of Management, 19*, 595-612.

Ogilvy, D. (2012). *Confessions of an advertising man.* London: Southbank.

Olechowski, N. (n.d.). *Why conversion isn't the only "best" metric.* Retrieved November 15, 2017, from https://retailnext.net/en/blog/best-retail-metric-conversion/

Oxford, J. (2013, September 24). *6 things online retailers can learn from Amazon.* Retrieved December 1, 2017, from http://www.forbes.com/sites/groupthink/2013/09/24/6-things-online-retailers-can-learn-from-amazon/

Patchen, M. (1965). *Some questionnaire measures of employee motivation and morale: A report on their reliability and validity, by Martin Patchen with the collaboration of Donald C. Pelz and Craig W. Allen.* Ann Arbor, MI: Survey Research Center Institute for Social Research University of Michigan.

Patzelt, H., & Shepherd, D.A. (2011). Recognizing opportunities for sustainable development. *Entrepreneurship Theory and Practice, 35*, 631-652.

Preston, J. (n.d.). *10 inspirational Richard Branson quotes.* Retrieved December 1, 2017, from http://www.virgin.com/entrepreneur/10-inspirational-richard-branson-quotes

Prive, T. (2013, May 5). *Top 32 quotes every entrepreneur should live by.* Retrieved December 1, 2017, from http://www.forbes.com/sites/tanyaprive/2013/05/02/top-32-quotes-every-entrepreneur-should-live-by/

Rauch, A., & Frese, M. (2000). Psychological approaches to entrepreneurial success: A general model and an overview of findings. In C.L. Cooper & I.T. Robertson (Eds.), *International review of industrial and organizational psychology, 15*(101-141). New York: John Wiley and Sons.

Rauch, A., & Frese, M. (2007). Let's put the person back into entrepreneurship research: A meta-analysis on the relationship between business owners' personality traits, business creation, and success. *European Journal of Work and Organizational Psychology*, *16*(4), 353-385.

Salter, C. (2008, February 19). *Marissa Mayer's 9 principles of innovation*. Retrieved December 1, 2017, from http://www.fastcompany.com/702926/marissa-mayers-9-principles-innovation

Sarasvathy, S.D. (2009). *Effectuation: Elements of entrepreneurial expertise*. Northampton, MA: Edward Elgar.

Schmidt, F.L., & Rader, M. (1999). Exploring the boundary conditions for interview validity: Meta-analytic validity findings for a new interview type. *Personnel Psychology*, *52*, 445-464.

Schmidt, F.L., & Rauschenberger, J. (1986). *Utility analysis for practitioners: A workshop*. First Annual Conference, Society for Industrial and Educational Psychology: Chicago, IL.

Shane, S. (2003). *A general theory of entrepreneurship: The individual-opportunity nexus approach to entrepreneurship*. Aldershot, UK: Edward Elgar.

Sharp, T. (2012, July 19). *World's first commercial airline: The greatest moments in flight*. Retrieved November 15, 2017, from https://www.space.com/16657-worlds-first-commercial-airline-the-greatest-moments-in-flight.html

Shaw, G., & Williams, A.M. (1998). Entrepreneurship, small business culture and tourism development. In D. Ioannides & K.G. Debbage (Eds.), *The economic geography of the tourist industry: A supply-side analysis*, 235-255. London: Routledge.

Shen, Y., Cotton, R.D., & Kram, K.E. (2015, March 16). Assembling your personal board of advisors. *MIT Sloan Management Review*, *56*(3).

Simon, M., Houghton, S.M., & Aquino, K. (1999). Cognitive biases, risk perception, and venture formation: How individuals decide to start companies. *Journal of Business Venturing*, *15*, 113-134.

Smith-Hunter, A., Kapp, J., & Yonkers, V. (2003). A psychological model of entrepreneurial behavior. *Journal of Academy of Business and Economics*, *2*, 180-192.

Society for Industrial and Organizational Psychology, Inc. (2003). *Principles for the validation and use of personnel selection procedures* (4th ed.). Bowling Green, OH: Author.

Sorensen, J.B. (2007). Closure and exposure: Mechanisms in the intergenerational transmission of self-employment. *Research in the Sociology of Organizations*, *25*, 83-124.

SRI/Gallup. (1989). *The process of new venture creation: How to set it up and make it work*.

Stenner, T. (2017, March 26). *The secret to success? Intellectual curiosity.* Retrieved December 1, 2017, from https://beta.theglobeandmail.com/globe-investor/investment-ideas/the-secret-to-success-intellectual-curiosity/article4217614/?ref=http://www.theglobeandmail.com&

Stewart, B. (2011, September 7). *The human internet.* Retrieved December 1, 2017, from http://utahvalleybusinessq.com/cover-stories/the-human-internet/

Stewart, W.H., & Roth, P.L. (2004). Data quality affects meta-analytic conclusions: A response to Miner and Raju (2004) concerning entrepreneurial risk propensity. *Journal of Applied Psychology, 89*, 14-21.

Taylor, B. (2012, April 4). *It's not what you sell, it's what you believe.* Retrieved December 1, 2017, from http://blogs.hbr.org/2012/04/its-not-what-you-sell-its-what/

Taylor, H.C., & Russell, J.T. (1939). The relationship of validity coefficients to the practical effectiveness of tests in selection: Discussion and tables. *Journal of Applied Psychology, 23*, 565-578.

Tett, R.P., & Burnett, D.D. (2003). A personality trait-based interactionist model of job performance. *Journal of Applied Psychology, 88*(3), 500-517.

Timmons, J.A. (1994). *New venture creation (4th ed.).* Burr Ridge, IL: Irwin.

Trefis Team. (2015, January 2). *Charles Schwab's year in review: Asset management, interest revenues, trading in focus.* Retrieved November 20, 2017, from https://www.forbes.com/sites/greatspeculations/2015/01/02/charles-schwabs-year-in-review-asset-management-interest-revenues-trading-in-focus/#408298f17f3a

Underemployment. (2017, November 8). In *Merriam-Webster.* Retrieved November 8, 2017, from https://www.merriam-webster.com/dictionary/underemployment

Uzzi, B. (March 1997). Social structure and competition in interfirm networks: The paradox of embeddedness. *Administrative Science Quarterly, 42*(1), 35-67.

von, Z., Dabiri, G., & Truscott-Smith, A. (2009). Naturtalent stiftung: Entrepreneur index development study.

Wooton, K.C., & Timmerman, T.A. (1999). The use of personality and the five factor model to predict business ventures: From outplacement to start-up. *Journal of Vocational Behavior, 58*, 82-101.

Zelman, J. (2011, October 5). *(Founder Stories) Meetup's Heiferman to founders: "Avoid thinking you have to do it all."* Retrieved December 1, 2017, from http://techcrunch.com/2011/10/05/founder-stories-meetups-heiferman-to-founders-avoid/

REFERENCES

Zero minus sixteen and counting. An address by John R. Evans, Commissioner, Securities and Exchange Commission, Washington, D.C. (April 15, 1975) (testimony of John R. Evans). Retrieved November 8, 2017, from http://3197d6d14b5f19f2f440-5e13d29c4c01 6cf96cbbfd197c579b45.r81.cf1.rackcdn.com/collection/papers/1970/1975_0415_ EvansZero.pdf

Zweig, J. (2015, April 30). The day Wall Street changed. *The Wall Street Journal.* Retrieved November 8, 2017, from https://blogs.wsj.com/moneybeat/2015/04/30/the-day-that-changed-wall-street-forever/?mg=id-wsj

Please note that any statistics not cited stem from Gallup research and studies.

ACKNOWLEDGEMENTS

We would like to thank everyone who made this book possible. It began with Don Clifton's pioneering theory of strengths and his focus on improving lives with greater emphasis on what's *right* with people rather than on what's wrong with them. His work of more than five decades, which included his focus on the psychology of the entrepreneur, became the foundation for the Builder Profile 10 (BP10) assessment and this book. Our deepest gratitude to Don for teaching us to soar with our strengths.

Many have generously given their time and talent to develop the entrepreneurship initiative at Gallup. Many thanks to Todd Johnson and Joe Daly for their leadership and their tireless commitment to Gallup's Entrepreneurship and Job Creation practice. Our sincere thanks to Jim Krieger, Steve O'Brien and Phil Ruhlman for their invaluable wisdom, big-picture thinking and unwavering belief in this project.

A very special thanks to Gerardo Aranda and his team for leading the charge in Mexico, advancing the entrepreneurial mindset among hundreds of thousands of high school students and helping thousands of startups and small businesses become sustainable and more productive. Many thanks to Scott Wright and Bryant Ott for spending endless hours creating BP10 reports and deliverables. We would also like to thank our technology experts — Emily Ternus, Jiear Rueschhoff and Kelly Slater — for designing the online platform and crafting the perfect content for the website.

This book would not have been possible without Geoff Brewer, editor extraordinaire, who deftly merged two author voices into a coherent narrative, and Seth Schuchman and the entire team at Gallup Press for navigating the deep and sometimes choppy waters of publishing with ease and élan while maintaining the highest levels of quality throughout the production process.

We are grateful to the reviewers, Steve O'Brien, Jon Clifton, Connie Rath, Brandon Busteed, Jim Harter, Mark Pogue, Tom Nolan and Todd Johnson, for their valuable feedback and constructive comments on the early drafts of this manuscript. Thanks to Kelly Henry for her masterful editing and collaboration on multiple text rewrites, to Trista Kunce for her patient and thorough fact checking of several drafts, and to Samantha Allemang for her aesthetic book design. Huge thanks go to Chin-Yee Lai for another striking Gallup Press book cover. And thanks to Tim Dean for keeping all of us in line and on task, moving from one milestone to the next in perfect harmony, and to Christine Sheehan for all of her support and partnership throughout.

This work would not have been possible without the cumulative brilliance and knowledge of our exceptionally talented psychologists and scientists. First and foremost, thanks to Joe Streur, Principal Psychologist and Consultant, Workplace Management, and Rajesh Srinivasan, Global Director of Research — World Poll, with whom we have had the extraordinary good fortune to collaborate and learn from while developing the BP10 assessment. We would also like to thank the following experts for their help, comments and suggestions: Frank L. Schmidt, Professor Emeritus at the Department of Management and Organizations, Tippie College of Business, University of Iowa; Jim Harter, Chief Scientist of Workplace Management at Gallup; Jim Asplund, Chief Scientist for Gallup's Strengths Practice; and Yongwei Yang, former Principal Researcher for Methodology and Predictive Analytics at Gallup.

Many thanks to all the builders who generously shared their experiences as successful entrepreneurs with us. Their quotes and insights dot the book — as do the learnings from hundreds of thousands of builders across the U.S. who completed the BP10 assessment and allowed us to research and study their talents.

Finally, we would like thank our families for their endless patience and support through long months of book writing. And thanks to our colleagues and friends at Gallup for inspiring us to continue the strengths journey.

ABOUT THE AUTHORS

Jim Clifton is Chairman and CEO of Gallup and author of *The Coming Jobs War*. His most recent innovation, the Gallup World Poll, is designed to give the world's 7 billion citizens a voice in virtually all key global issues. Under Clifton's leadership, Gallup has expanded from a predominantly U.S.-based company to a worldwide organization with 40 offices in 30 countries and regions.

Sangeeta Badal, Ph.D., is the principal scientist for Gallup's Builder Initiative. Dr. Badal is responsible for translating research findings into interventions that drive small-business growth. She is the author of the book *Gender, Social Structure and Empowerment: Status Report of Women in India*. Dr. Badal earned her doctorate in anthropology and geography from the University of Nebraska.

Gallup Press exists to educate and inform the people who govern, manage, teach and lead the world's 7 billion citizens. Each book meets Gallup's requirements of integrity, trust and independence and is based on Gallup-approved science and research.